LAUREN BACALL

HOLLYWOOD LEGENDS SERIES
CARL ROLLYSON, GENERAL EDITOR

LAUREN BACALL

THE QUEEN OF COOL

ANTHONY UZAROWSKI

UNIVERSITY PRESS OF MISSISSIPPI / JACKSON

The University Press of Mississippi is the scholarly publishing agency of the Mississippi Institutions of Higher Learning: Alcorn State University, Delta State University, Jackson State University, Mississippi State University, Mississippi University for Women, Mississippi Valley State University, University of Mississippi, and University of Southern Mississippi.

www.upress.state.ms.us

The University Press of Mississippi is a member of the Association of University Presses.

Photo on page ii courtesy Album / Alamy Stock Photo

Manufactured in the United States of America

∞

Publisher: University Press of Mississippi, Jackson, USA
Authorised GPSR Safety Representative: Easy Access System Europe - Mustamäe tee 50, 10621 Tallinn, Estonia, gpsr.requests@easproject.com

Hardback ISBN 978-1-4968-3883-4
Epub single ISBN 978-1-4968-6110-8
Epub institutional ISBN 978-1-4968-6111-5
PDF single ISBN 978-1-4968-6112-2
PDF institutional ISBN 978-1-4968-6113-9

British Library Cataloging-in-Publication Data available

TO ALL THE FRIENDS ENCOUNTERED ON THE ROAD, PAST AND FUTURE.

IN MEMORY OF MY FATHER.

Wide-mouthed, with a deep deadeye voice—sounding sexy and faintly mad-at-someone, Lauren Bacall looks the way most American women yearn to look; the way that stops men—American and otherwise—smack in their tracks.

—*VOGUE*, NOVEMBER 15, 1959

CONTENTS

PREFACE AND ACKNOWLEDGMENTS

LAUREN BACALL, OR BETTY, AS SHE WAS KNOWN TO FRIENDS, WAS ONE OF the emblematic stars of the Golden Age of Hollywood. Her career spanned seven decades and was one of the longest and most distinguished in the history of show business. Yet it wasn't an easy career: after becoming a star at nineteen with her first film, *To Have and Have Not* in 1944, she later joked that there was nowhere for her to go but down. She became an icon of film noir before the term was even invented: a cool, sophisticated, sexy, and ultramodern woman, she projected confidence and independence. Over the years, the type of parts she played changed, and as she moved from Hollywood to Broadway in the 1960s, she managed to establish a new career at a time when most of her contemporaries faded into oblivion. Critical appraisal of her work varied, but what remained constant throughout the years was her undeniable star power which kept audiences fascinated, no matter what project Bacall was involved in.

Lauren Bacall worked into old age, never resting on her laurels, always challenging herself. Her work remained fresh and modern, and as she moved into the new millennium, she appeared in a diverse range of projects across different media. From being directed by Lars von Trier to voicing a character in *Family Guy*, Bacall kept herself relevant to a degree no other classic Hollywood movie star ever had. And yet it was impossible to ever forget that she was also the same iconic figure who had set the screen ablaze opposite Humphrey Bogart decades earlier.

Her relationship with Bogart is the stuff of legend, the most beloved pairing of classical Hollywood, a perfect blend of romance, glamour, and cinematic glory. When Bogart died in 1957, Bacall was merely thirty-three years old, and for the rest of her life, she would wrestle with the legend of her late husband, struggling to prove to the industry and the public that she was more than just the most famous widow in Hollywood. In the end, she managed to achieve that, becoming a two-time Tony Award–winning Broadway star, a bestselling author, and continuing a successful, though at times rocky, screen career, which brought her an Academy Award nomination in 1996 and an Honorary Oscar in 2009. In 1999, the American Film Institute included Bacall in their list of fifty greatest screen legends of all time.

Lauren Bacall's presence is woven into the very fabric of twentieth-century American culture, and yet, until now, there have been no books, academic or otherwise, solely dedicated to the exploration of her long and complex career. My aim was to bring the reader closer to knowing Bacall the actor, the artist, and the creator of her iconic image, as well as the woman behind the legend. Bacall revealed much about her life in her two very well-written books, and her life with Bogart was covered thoroughly in William J. Mann's 2023 book, *Bogie and Bacall.* What interested me most about Bacall was not her life in relation to Bogart; I believe her artistic legacy is highly deserving of close analysis and that Bacall herself is a fascinating enough subject to merit a book that focuses squarely on her, not only on her marriage. This is not so much a definitive biography as it is an in-depth look at a unique movie star and the cultural landscape in which she operated.

Bacall was fiercely protective of her privacy; she never believed that she owed the public anything beyond her work and what she chose to share. In writing this book, I wanted to be respectful of her memory, as well as of her three children. Stephen, Leslie, and Sam politely declined to be interviewed for this work, as they did for William J. Mann's book and the majority of other projects focusing on their famous parents. I fully understand and respect their decision—after all, they've had to wrestle with the Bogart/Bacall/Robards legends all their lives.

The following is a portrait of Lauren Bacall—not of "Bogie's Baby" or "the Look" or "the Voice." She was a complex woman—flawed, temperamental, lovable, talented, at times deeply insecure and difficult, always fascinating. Many of her struggles which I have tried to shed light on touch upon wider issues of the times she lived in. Jewish identity, feminism, gender roles, political divisions, the construction of our collective cultural memory, the standards of beauty and style, and aging femininity—Bacall's story is intertwined with all these crucial concepts.

"I don't do things for posterity," she once said. "Once I'm gone, that's it, as far as I'm concerned." Yet her legacy is enormous—not only as a screen star but also as a woman who defied the patriarchal structure and lived life very much on her own terms.

Writing this book in many places around the world—from London and Paris to California and Southeast Asia—has been a great adventure. I owe a debt of gratitude to the many people whose help, patience, and generous assistance made it all possible. Thank you to the staff of the Margaret Herrick Library in Los Angeles, the British Film Institute and the British Library in London, and the American Library in Paris. I have found many hidden treasures in your collections and your kindness has been invaluable. Thanks also to Michael Gregg Michaud for your memories, photographs, and friendship. To Nat Segaloff, Fred Goldrich, Dan Callahan, Benjamin Meißner, Greta Ritchie, Andy Budgell, Jeremy Kinser, Lucy Bolton, and the late, great Jay Jorgensen. Thank you to Sidsel Robards for your efforts. And to Henry Bink for sharing your immense collection of newspaper and magazine articles on Bacall with me.

To Emily Bandy and everyone at the University Press of Mississippi: thank you for creating such a nurturing and generous environment any author would be lucky to work in and for giving Lauren Bacall a good home. To my agent, Lee Sobel: we've done it again.

To the people I'm so lucky to have in my life, thank you for your love and support: Kendra Bean, Steph Brandhuber, Olivia Doutney, Tony Walsh, Abaigh Wheatley, and Greg Windle. To Dream and Millie at

CoCoCo Phayam—the most welcoming and magical place any writer could envisage. And last but not least, to my partner Sylvain, for lovingly sharing this journey with me.

LAUREN BACALL

CHAPTER 1

Betty

SHE WAS A CHILD OF THE ROARING TWENTIES, A DAUGHTER TO A NEW YORK City which exists today only in the flickering, black-and-white images preserved on old film reels. Her New York was not the city of old families and society balls, Park Avenue, and the stock market. Hers was the New York of immigrants, those who had come from faraway places, yearning for freedom, for opportunity, for a new start. Their drive and ambition would seep into her blood, too. Her people worked hard, adapted fast, didn't feel sorry for themselves. They took root as soon as they planted their feet on American soil, and they climbed fiercely toward the sun, through the unforgiving jungle of this new world.

Her parents were Jewish. Her father, William Perske, came from an ancient line of Polish Jews, originating in the Wolozyn region in the eastern part of Poland (today, the city of Valozhyn in Belarus). The family name had been originally spelled Perski—upon William's parents' arrival in America in the 1880s, the spelling was changed to Persky, and it would eventually become Perske. It was a family of some distinction: merchants and scholars, speaking multiple languages. Back in Poland, they'd been a part of a thriving Jewish community; more than half of Wolozyn's population were at the time Jewish. Increasing tensions with the occupying Russian Empire, which imposed anti-Jewish laws, and the growing antisemitism forced many families to flee and journey across the ocean, with hopes for a better future. Hyman and Betsy (also sometimes referred to as Bessy or Rebecca) Persky settled in New Jersey, where their son, William, was born in 1889. They later moved to Brooklyn, where Hyman started a tailoring business, and where they'd have two more children, Augusta and Elsie.

William grew up to be a man of many dreams. He was handsome, by all accounts possessing the same kind of allure which would one day make his daughter world famous. He worked his way up the pharmaceutics and medical equipment business, establishing his own drugstore by the early 1920s. Around the same time, he had fallen in love with Natalie Weinstein-Bacal, a Jewish émigré from Romania, twelve years his junior. The Weinstein-Bacals had arrived in New York in 1904, via Ellis Island, where their name was recorded only as Weinstein. Natalie had just turned three. Her parents, Max and Sophie, hailed from Iasi, the cultural heart of Romania, at the time, home to a large Jewish population. Max was a modest wheat farmer, with a wife and three small children to support—Renee, Natalie, and Albert, all born between 1900 and the end of 1902. 1903 proved to be the year when things came to a head for the family. The wheat crop failed; the antisemitic laws meant that no government aid was granted to help them. Like many other Eastern European Jews, including the Perskis, the Weinstein-Bacals felt they had little choice but to leave the only home they'd ever known and head to America, the new promised land. Money was incredibly short, with the first few years in the States a constant struggle for survival. In the meantime, two more children were added to the family: Charles in 1905, and Jack a year later. These years of hardship would come to be forever after symbolized by "the pushcart"—the unmentionable and yet omnipresent memory of Max and his pushcart, filled with household goods for sale, wandering the streets of downtown New York, trying to provide for his family. In time, things would improve—the American dream kicked in—as Max was able to move the family to an apartment in the Bronx and open his own candy store. He would die suddenly, aged just fifty-five, but he had achieved what he fought so hard for: his family was safe and relatively secure.

Charlie and Jack attended night school at City College, both eventually obtaining law degrees, while their mother, Sophie, continued to expand the store with the help of her older children. Natalie found work as a secretary, and when, in 1922, she married William Persky, a successful pharmacist, it seemed like the family fortunes were truly on the rise.

But the marital bliss didn't last. Natalie and William were not a happy couple, with cracks in their relationship showing from the start. Within the first year of marriage, William's business also suffered. Persky was arrested for illegally selling morphine, and although the case was eventually settled, he was banned from operating his drugstore for the duration of the trial, which severely affected the family finances. Soon after, Natalie became pregnant. The circumstances were less than ideal but Natalie decided that this baby would be a source of joy, no matter what else was to unfold.

On a warm evening in early fall, Natalie took herself to the movies. The magical, silent images flickered before her. It was still a new medium, one everyone, regardless of where they had come from and what language they spoke, could enjoy. Suddenly, Natalie felt a pain, and she knew it was time. In retrospect, it seems rather fitting that her baby would choose a movie screening to signal her entrance into the world. Hours later, in the Bronx Lebanon Hospital, Betty Joan Persky was born. It was September 24, 1924.

From the very beginning, the bond between Natalie and her daughter was incredibly tight. The baby became a beacon of hope and a reason to live. For the first five years of Betty's life, the Perskes tried to keep their marriage going. Decades later, Betty (by then Lauren), would remember her parents' fights, describing her father as a volatile, jealous man. "In all fairness, how does a child of three, or four, or five know what goes on between a man and a woman?" she wrote in her memoir. By 1930, things apparently got bad enough for Natalie to say, enough is enough. It couldn't have been an easy decision for her to make. The stock market had crashed just months before, the country was in the grips of a depression. It would not be easy for a single mother to keep things afloat. One day, she took little Betty, packed all their things, and left the Brooklyn apartment they'd shared as a family for the past few years. When William Perske (he had changed the spelling of their surname sometime after his trial) returned home later that day, he had a message waiting for him, delivered by the building's superintendent: "Your wife told me to tell you she's not coming back to you. She's leaving you."

Accounts differ regarding Perske's subsequent involvement in his daughter's life—according to Lauren's recollections, she continued to see her father every Sunday until the age of eight. Then, one weekend, he brought her back home, drove off, and left her life for good. He was never to reappear. This would put the date of his last visit at around 1932—the same year in which Perske moved to Washington, DC, which would confirm Lauren's version. Many years later, William Perske would attempt to clear his name, presenting his own version of events to the press. In 1979, after the release of Lauren's memoir, *By Myself*, Perske gave an interview to the *Los Angeles Times*. According to his memory, he had never seen Betty after the day Natalie left their Brooklyn apartment, the same day on which he allegedly left his daughter at a summer camp. "From the day I sent Betty to camp, I have not seen her," he told the journalist. "I tried to see her, but her mother wouldn't let me see her. So, I moved out of town and came to Washington in 1932."

"She never tried to turn me against my father," Lauren would write about her mother. "She was too busy going about the business of making a living, paying the rent, feeding, and clothing me." The absence of her father, which she called "rejection number one," would come to shape her life in more ways than one. Her anger and disappointment in him would persist for decades; she never forgave him or was able to face him, even when years later, after her Hollywood success, Perske resurfaced and tried to contact her. In later decades, he would try again. "When her play was in Washington, I wanted to talk to her," he recalled in 1979. She said, "I hardly know you." I said, "Well, how can you know me if you won't see me? There is another side. You should hear what I have to say and form your own conclusion." But the meeting would never take place. William Perske died in 1982, without ever reuniting with his daughter. Writer Richard Cohen, who would later become Lauren's friend, met Perske not long before his death. William wanted, once again, to tell his side of the story. Cohen remembered arriving at the lobby of Perske's apartment building, where he was to be met by the man himself.

"I asked how I would recognize him," Cohen recalled. "That, he said, would not be a problem. Boy, was he right! The man in the lobby was Lauren Bacall, had she been born a man and had aged some. He had her face, all the features pointing down, sultry and aquiline —all in all, totally Bacallish."

William retold his story to Cohen, the same one he had to the *Los Angeles Times*: "He denied that he had ever abandoned his family. He said his wife had left him. He said it was not likely that his daughter knew the truth." Cohen printed the story, but, as he later noted, "I didn't necessarily believe him, but I did not disbelief him either. My point was that the truth no longer mattered. He was a mere man, and his daughter was no longer Betty Joan Perske, but Lauren Bacall, movie star. Her version of what happened—false or not—was the truth. His rebuttal, his meager protest, was just a chirp in a boiler factory."

• • •

After the breakup of the Perske marriage, Natalie and Betty moved to Manhattan, and Natalie took back her family name—or at least, the second part of it—and became Natalie Bacal. Betty, who had already by then harbored dreams of becoming a dancer or actress, was happy with the change. Betty Bacal would look better on a marquee. She lived in the world of her own imagination, with romantic dreams and grand plans for the future. Natalie encouraged her daughter's ambitions. Despite modest finances, she enrolled Betty in dance classes. For a time, Betty was a boarder at the Highland Manor school for girls in New Jersey, where she excelled in sports and was a bright student—so much so that she was allowed to skip a grade and graduate a year before her peers. During her time at Highland Manor, Betty's theatrical dreams took serious shape. She was involved in all the school's performances—dramas, musicals, dance recitals—and by the time she graduated, she was convinced that the stage was her destiny. There had been no precedence for this kind of career choice—no one in the family had ever been involved in anything even remotely related to show business. After leaving Highland Manor, Betty returned to Manhattan to live with Natalie. They would share a small apartment on Eighty-fourth Street and West End Avenue with Grandma Sophie and Uncle Charlie, both of whom Betty adored. With her father gone from her life, Natalie's brothers, Charlie and Jack, became incredibly important to Betty. Their support throughout her childhood, both financial and emotional, was something she'd come to recognize in her adult life as a great gift, crucial to her eventual success.

Uncle Charlie appeared to Betty a very worldly man; he was well-educated, handsome, with a great sense of humor. He encouraged her to keep abreast of current events and to read the *New York Times*. Like Betty's mother, Charlie stressed the importance of honesty and character. Uncle Jack, who now went by Jacques Bacal, an important lawyer with many friends in high places, was another major influence. Even if Natalie's means were modest—at the time she worked as a secretary and a housekeeper—growing up under the influence of her uncles, Betty acquired an air of sophistication which in later years would sometimes lead people to assume she had come from a wealthy, WASPy family. Her Jewish heritage and Eastern European roots were not central to her identity. It wasn't uncommon for first-generation immigrants to focus on integration rather than dwell on what had been left behind. Betty's only link to her family's past was Sophie, who instilled in her granddaughter some of the wisdom and tradition from the Old World. Sophie was the only one in the family to uphold religious rituals. She lit a candle every Friday in memory of her late husband

and attended Temple. Young Betty didn't think much about what being Jewish meant, or how it could set her apart from others.

Betty enrolled at Julia Richman High School, an all-girls school on the Upper East Side, which had the advantage of being tuition-free. She remained a good student, but with her mind constantly preoccupied with dreams of a stage career, she had little interest in other subjects. For a time, she continued her dance classes under the instructions of the renowned Russian dancer Mikhail Mordkin. Although Betty had dedication, at the end of the school year Mordkin told Natalie that her daughter would never be an exceptional ballet dancer, and since money continued to be short, it made sense to stop. With one dream shattered, Betty could focus all of her attention on acting. On Saturday mornings, she took drama classes at the New York School of the Theatre. "I had my first taste of improvisation, of memorizing scenes, playing parts of all ages," she later remembered. She looked forward to those Saturday morning classes all week. At Julia Richman, she also exhibited talent for writing when she signed up for a journalism class—a class she took after being inspired by Rosalind Russell in *His Girl Friday*. Growing up with a working mother and observing her uncles, both successful professional men, Betty developed a strong work ethic. She knew the value of hard work and saw work as something that gave one's life meaning—it wasn't just about paying the bills and making ends meet. Dedicating oneself to a profession one was passionate about, and doing it well, was a noble, worthwhile pursuit. For her, that work would be acting. Not everyone was thrilled about her choice. Sophie, for one, found the idea of her beloved granddaughter going into the shady world of the theater to be appalling. But Natalie was adamant in her support—if Betty wanted to pursue acting, that's what she would do.

After graduating from high school, Betty auditioned and was accepted at the American Academy of Dramatic Arts, a private drama school in Manhattan that bore the distinction of being the oldest acting school in the English-speaking world. Fees were quite high, and Betty was grateful that her uncles agreed to cover them, at least for the first year. Uncle Jack gave her yet another reason to be grateful. He knew of her fascination—if not obsession—with Bette Davis. Betty had seen all of Davis's films, many times over. She would imitate the star, repeating her iconic lines, her walk, her way of speaking. It was no secret to anyone in the family that Bette Davis meant the world to Betty. It just so happened that one of Uncle Jack's friends was also close to Davis, who, upon visiting New York in the spring of 1940, agreed to meet Betty and her best friend at her hotel suite. It was no small thing for a busy movie star from Hollywood to agree to a meeting with two star-struck kids—but friends are friends, and Davis was known as a good sport. This was beyond anything Betty had dared to dream of: meeting her idol in the flesh, sitting beside her, talking to her. In later years, she'd remember Davis as patient and kind, and the encounter as a profound gift, which had greatly impacted her young self. "No crown of diamonds placed on the head of a fairy princess by a handsome prince could mean as much," she wrote. She couldn't have predicted that a mere five years later she would be Davis's colleague at Warner Bros.

"My days were full and near perfect that year," Lauren Bacall would one day write about her time at the American Academy of Dramatic Arts. After years of diluting her attention with subjects she had little interest in, she was now allowed to pour all of her energy in a single direction. She threw herself into studying her craft—speech, movement, improvisation, writing and performing monologues. Back to dance, her first love. And of course, acting with other students. Betty found herself nervous and self-conscious before each performance, but she slowly gained confidence. The mystery of acting fascinated her, and she couldn't get enough.

Friday evenings at the Academy were her favorite. The senior students would put on plays in the Carnegie Lyceum Theatre, located in the basement of the Academy's building, and the freshmen students were allowed to sit in, watch, and learn. One young actor stood out from the rest, at least to Betty. Strikingly handsome, with piercing blue eyes, blond hair, and a cleft chin, she thought him "marvelous—so attractive and so good." He later introduced himself as Kirk Douglas. Betty was sixteen at the time, and Douglas, twenty-four. She was full of romantic fantasies, and for a time, Kirk became the leading man in all of them. They went out to eat and see movies, and Betty introduced him to her family. He told her how poor he had been—the Academy had offered him a scholarship based on his exceptional talent—and she gave him one of Uncle Charlie's old coats to keep himself warm during those bitter winter blizzards. To Betty's disappointment, their friendship would remain just that; Douglas was in love with his Academy classmate, Diana Dill, whom he would eventually marry.

At the end of the school year, Betty did her final performance—her grades were good, but she was not offered the scholarship she had hoped for. Natalie couldn't afford to pay the Academy's tuition for the second year—even with her brothers' support—and so Betty would have to abandon her education. It was a disappointing blow, but it didn't deter her from following her dream. After months of being around other actors, of seeing them work, she wanted it more than ever.

Leaving school meant getting a job. With acting gigs still out of her reach, Betty turned to the next best thing—modeling. She didn't see herself as beautiful, certainly not in the same category as the stunning women she saw in the waiting room of the first studio she visited, but she apparently had enough confidence in her looks to tell the interviewing woman she had been a photographic model for years. Since she was still only sixteen, it's unlikely the woman believed her, but she was impressed enough to give the young girl a chance. For thirty dollars a week, a considerable sum at the time, Betty Bacal began her first real job, modeling clothes for David Crystal on Seventh Avenue. It was spring, 1941, and by the end of the summer, she was told she wouldn't be needed anymore. Was it because she had told the other girls she was Jewish? It was the first time in her life she was made aware of her Jewish identity as something that set her apart and that could lead to discrimination. The fact she apparently "didn't look Jewish" and people's surprise at finding out all made her feel terribly uncomfortable and even more self-conscious than she had already been. She wasn't equipped to deal with prejudice. Her family had experienced it back in Europe, it had been the thing that pushed them out of their ancestral home, but there was never any talk about it at home—she had no guidebook to follow.

She would soon find other modeling gigs, but it was still the theater that continued to be her focus. With no agent and no experience, the chances of landing a role in a play were slim. She started hanging out outside Sardi's, the Mecca of Broadway, selling issues of *Actor's Cue*, a pamphlet that listed theater jobs. She'd approach Broadway producers, whose faces she had seen in the papers, offer to sell them a copy of the *Actor's Cue*, and ask about roles in their upcoming plays. "I really was crazy, now that I think of it," she would write years later. "But it was fun to do. My face became familiar to important producers, which all helped, since when I went to their offices when plays were being cast, at least they recognized me when they said no."

She did eventually get lucky, winning a walk-on part in the Broadway production of *Johnny 2 X 4*, which opened in March 1942. The show was panned by critics, closing after less than two months, but it didn't matter. It was her first professional acting engagement—even if it was barely a part at all, it was Broadway, and Betty was over the moon. She signed her contract as Betty Bacall—for the first time adding an extra "L" and thus making it easier for people to pronounce it correctly. She was now a member of Actor's Equity—part of that fabled guild of storytellers and crazy dreamers she felt she belonged with, with all her heart. Later the same year, she got cast in an uncredited role in the great Max Gordon's production of *Franklin Street*, to star Groucho Marx. She was thrilled, believing she had finally hit the big time. To her great disappointment, the play turned out to be a dismal failure, closing out of town before it ever had the chance to reach Broadway.

Throughout this period, Betty also worked as a theater usher on Broadway. It wasn't exactly the sort of theater work she had hoped for, but it did mean a continued connection to the stage and a chance of being seen. It also meant the opportunity to see plays nightly, for free, as well as a small paycheck. By this point, Betty and Natalie were living on Bank Street in Greenwich Village, and with money being short, as ever, any financial contribution from Betty was greatly welcomed.

That May, Betty was crowned "Miss Greenwich Village," which was accompanied by a small amount of publicity, including photos of the smiling seventeen-year-old in the local press.

She had certainly had a busy couple of years. All of the experiences she'd amassed might have not amounted to much in terms of getting cast in plays, but she had pulled on so many strings of fate that something good was bound to come of it. She believed it, and so did Natalie. Neither could have predicted just how fast destiny's dominos would fall, and how far they were about to carry her.

• • •

"She came into my office, with that big smile, wide Russian face—I don't know how keen she'd be to be called a Russian, but that's what she looked like to me in those days." That's how Diana Vreeland recalled her first meeting with Betty Bacall, many decades after it had occurred. Vreeland, herself a legendary figure, would from that day on be inextricably linked to the legend of Lauren Bacall. How did the seventeen-year-old unknown get to meet Diana Vreeland, the chief fashion editor at *Harper's Bazaar*? It was certainly an unlikely meeting, a clash of two very different worlds. Vreeland was old money, a socialite born in Paris, whose life was, in her own words, made up of "traveling, seeing beautiful places, having marvelous summers, studying and reading a great deal of the time." At least, that's the way it had been before 1936, the year she joined the staff of *Harper's*. Vreeland had a definitive vision for her fashion spreads. Her opinions and the advice she showered on her readers were often eccentric, but few would dare to disagree with her. In her memoir, Lauren called Vreeland "definitely an original."

The introduction was arranged by Nicolas de Gunzburg, himself a Paris-born editor at *Harper's Bazaar*, who, struck by Betty's youthful beauty, insisted that she be brought before Vreeland. In her book, Lauren recalls meeting de Gunzburg through an English writer whom she names as Timothy Brooke. No clear records of Timothy Brooke, the writer, exist, suggesting the name might have been an alias. Bacall remembered the middle-aged Brooke as "very charming and funny" and a "great deal older" than herself, and while there was no attraction on her part, they "got along well." Brooke took Betty around to some of Manhattan's fashionable clubs, places she couldn't have afforded to go into by herself. It was at one of such clubs, a place called Tony's, that Brooke introduced Betty to his old friend, Nicky de Gunzburg.

What did he, and subsequently Vreeland, see in the young Betty Bacall? Her own appraisal of herself was painfully self-deprecating. "I was flat chested, larger-foot, very gawky, I was always shy to smile because my teeth were crooked—God, I don't know, I was a mess," she joked decades later. And yet within minutes of meeting her, Vreeland had no doubt that this girl had something special. She arranged for her to be seen the following day by her collaborator and *Harper's* head fashion photographer, Louise Dahl-Wolfe, who took numerous test snaps of Betty. "I was a basket case of nerves," Bacall later wrote. She was wearing no makeup and was pale—this was November in New York City, after all. Dahl-Wolfe was greatly impressed by what she saw later in her darkroom.

"You can't get a bad picture of Bacall," she would one day reflect. "There's nothing eccentric about her. She's perfect all over and yet she looks like nobody else." Vreeland had a similar impression: "Betty was great. You couldn't take a bad picture of her. Not possibly take a bad picture. I've never seen a model quite like that." It was clear that the camera loved her—at least, the still camera. The two women quickly agreed that Betty Bacall was perfect for their shared vision of *Harper's Bazaar*. And so began the brief but crucial period of Bacall's life. She only modeled for *Harper's* for less than five months, between November 1942 and March 1943, and yet the photographs Dahl-Wolfe took of her during this period would come to alter the course of destiny.

Dahl-Wolfe photographed her in elegant Manhattan apartments, including one owned by Helena Rubinstein. There were shots of her wearing some of the season's latest fashions, snaps of her in a bathing suit perched on the edge of a huge bathtub. She looked mysterious, glamorous, sophisticated—all the things she wasn't. "None of it was me," she would tell Michael Parkinson. "What can you be when you're eighteen years old (in fact she was still seventeen), know nothing, you have no life experience—how sophisticated can you be for heaven's sake?" But it's what the camera saw with its magical eye, not reality, that mattered. The first picture of Bacall appeared inside the January 1943 issue of *Harper's Bazaar*, which landed on the nation's newsstands in late December. A month later, Vreeland showed Betty the February issue: she was featured, once again, inside the magazine, but this time she was named as "an actress"—though her name had been misspelled as "Betty Becall." It was likely this issue which caught the eye of Slim Hawks, the wife of Hollywood director Howard Hawks.

While part of Bacall's legend is that Mrs. Hawks saw her on the cover of *Harper's Bazaar*, in reality the now-iconic shot of Betty standing by the Red Cross door would appear on the cover only in March 1943—by this time Hawks, as well as a number of other Hollywood people, had already been in touch with Vreeland. Among them was David O. Selznick, who had famously "discovered" Vivien Leigh as the perfect Scarlett O'Hara for his epic adaptation of *Gone with the Wind*. Columbia Pictures wanted Bacall to appear in their upcoming production, *Cover Girl*, which was to star Rita Hayworth. Betty would likely have a small cameo as the "*Harper's Bazaar* Girl." And then, there was the enquiry from Charles Feldman, who was Howard Hawks's agent. Hawks was an esteemed director, and Betty had already seen many of his films, including *Only Angels Have Wings* and *Bringing Up Baby*. Feldman told Natalie that Hawks had been greatly impressed with her pictures and that he wanted to bring her to California for a screen test. If he liked her, she'd be signed to a personal contract with the director. That meant she'd get his personal attention, he'd work with her, make sure she was cast in parts which best showcased her talents. Uncle Jack, who as an entertainment lawyer, was seen by the whole family as an authority, advised Betty to accept Hawks's offer. Vreeland, thinking of the magazine, wanted Betty to represent *Harper's* in the Columbia picture, but she had to agree that for the good of her career, she had to do what she felt was right. The decision was made. Betty, not yet eighteen, would travel the three thousand miles west to California alone. How long she'd be gone, no one could know for sure. There were tears, an emotional goodbye with Natalie, with Sophie. The next time she'd return to New York City, she'd do so not as Betty Bacall, a shy unknown, but as Lauren Bacall, the star.

CHAPTER 2

The Whistle Heard Around the World

FEW ACTING DEBUTS IN THE HISTORY OF HOLLYWOOD HAVE HAD AN IMPACT comparable to that then there was the voice: low, husky, seductive, carrying with it mystery and sensual promise. Few among those who saw the film realized that the bundle of confident sexuality and sophistication they saw before them, this "woman-of-the-world," capable of out-cooling Humphrey Bogart, was in reality a nervous, innocent teenager, half the age of her leading man, who had to lower her chin in order to stop her head from shaking.

The road that led her to appearing in the film was itself like a story straight out of the movies. A famous director's wife spots a girl in a fashion magazine while having breakfast with her husband. She is struck by the young model's mysterious gaze and her confident poise. While there are hundreds of beautiful models in every issue of every fashion magazine, there is something distinctly different about this one. There's a story behind those catlike eyes, an invitation, or a challenge to know more about her. While sipping his coffee, Howard Hawks once again tells his wife about his dilemma. By this point, Hawks had been working on *To Have and Have Not* for nearly four years. Sometime in the early months of 1939 he had invited his buddy Ernest Hemingway on a fishing trip, with the intension of convincing Hemingway to write an original screenplay for Hawks to direct. Hemingway, with his famously disparaging attitude towards Hollywood, refused.

"Ernest, you're a damn fool," Hawks told the famed writer. "I can make a picture out of your worst story."

"What's my worst story?"

"That goddamn bunch of junk called *To Have and To Have Not* [*sic.*]"

Hemingway didn't believe that anything could be made of the story, but later that year he sold the film rights to the novel to another famous Howard, the producer and aviator Howard Hughes. During the months that followed, Hawks became convinced that he could indeed make a movie out of Hemingway's story; all he needed was a skilled writer who could transform the plot from overtly political and symbolic to more film-friendly entertainment. In 1943, Hawks finally managed to buy the rights from Hughes, and then sold them to Warner Bros., with the provision that he would be in total control of the picture. In exchange for their financial backing, Warners would get to distribute the film and cast their top leading man of the moment, Humphrey Bogart, in the central role of Captain Harry Morgan.

The string of writers Hawks hired to work on the screenplay changed Hemingway's story almost beyond recognition, adding characters, altering the plot, and even moving the location from Cuba to the Vichy-controlled Island of Martinique, where the context could be updated, from the Cuban Revolution of 1933 to current realities of World War II. By the spring of 1943, Hawks still wasn't completely satisfied with the script, but he was convinced it was headed in the right direction. This promised to be a film full of adventure, espionage, wartime heroism, and sex—a timely cocktail which Hawks hoped would bring audiences to the theaters. Alongside the hero, Harry Morgan, the story now also had a female lead. Warner Bros. was keen for Hawks to use one of their contract actresses, but for Hawks the presence of Bogart in the picture was enough—he didn't want the Warners stamp all over his film; this was to be his personal triumph. There was also something else brewing in his mind, an unfulfilled ambition, which he could now finally achieve. One of his fantasies had always been to discover an unknown girl and make her into a star, to mold and guide her, to be the creator of a myth. He was fascinated by the relationships of Greta Garbo and Mauritz Stiller and Marlene Dietrich and Josef von Sternberg: the idea of creating a goddess out of a mere mortal. This, however, was not an easy task. Goddesses didn't just come along whenever one wished for them, not even in Hollywood, and that spring morning, in the dining room of his Beverly Hills home, Hawks relayed his frustrations to his wife.

Nancy Keith, known to her wide circle of friends as Slim, was Hawks's second wife. She was noted for her impeccable style and sharp wit, and Hawks depended on her advice and expert eye for fashion, and for new faces. Slim had herself been a successful model, appearing on the cover of *Harper's Bazaar* at the age of twenty-two. And it was the February 1943 issue of *Harper's* that she was now carefully studying, perhaps seeing in the young girl something of herself—there was more than a passing resemblance between the two, a fact that didn't escape Hawks's attention either. That morning, he instructed his secretary to call New York and find out more about the mysterious model. In later years, Hawks maintained that at this stage he only wanted to find out more about Bacall, but that his secretary made a mistake and sent Betty a train ticket with a request to come out to California instead. That story is rather hard to believe, especially in the light of the fact that it took Betty and her family a good few days to accept the offer, during which Betty, her mother, Uncle Jack, and Diana Vreeland had all been in contact with Hawks's office. Even if Hawks wasn't fully aware of the whole situation, his agent, Charles Feldman, was in total control.

Feldman was one of the shrewdest agents in Hollywood, managing to operate largely outside the constraining rules of the studio system, befriending stars, developing scripts, and negotiating one-picture deals for freelance writers and actors. His background in law proved invaluable when it came to finding loopholes and exploitative clauses in the studio contracts, a skill which made Feldman particularly popular with the stars. Married to an ex-Ziegfeld Girl, Jean Howard, Feldman was also at the heart of Hollywood's social scene. Parties at the Feldmans, documented by Jean, who was a talented photographer, became legendary, attended by the who's who of the entertainment world and beyond. On Sunday afternoons, it was customary to gather by the pool, play games, and drink while discussing the latest gossip and business deals. In addition to the close connections he nurtured with established stars, Charlie was also famous for his unparalleled ability to spot potential new talent. He was instrumental in establishing the careers of many young actors and writers, always knowing which studio or director or project was in need of a fresh face before the camera or a talented writer to save a disastrous script behind the scenes.

By the early 1940s, Feldman realized that the public was hungry for a new kind of cinematic narrative. The impending doom of war that hung in the air changed the way audiences viewed films; light screwball comedies or lavish melodramatic plots of the 1930s suddenly felt irrelevant. A wave of Jewish directors, immigrating to the States to escape the Nazi persecution in Europe, brought a new flavor to American cinema—movies filled with a dark, atmospheric visual style and narratives that dealt with themes of alienation, crime, and disillusionment with modernity. Feldman knew that what these films needed was a new breed of stars to fit this dark, unsentimental reality and embody the characters who inhabited it. When Howard Hawks showed him the photos of Betty from the fateful issue of *Harper's Bazaar*, Feldman had an instant hunch that here was a girl who would feel right at home in this new cinematic reality. Could she act? And if not, could she learn? Feldman knew just what to do, and it seems that it was at this point that he took matters into his own hands.

In the following days, a series of telegrams were exchanged between Hollywood and New York; they were reassuring and full of promise, designed to woo the young model. Feldman knew that Hawks wasn't the only one in Hollywood to have noticed the *Harper's* girl. It was likely that at the very same time she was considering other offers, and it was his job to make his sound the most alluring. If signed to a personal contract, Betty would have the best possible care. Hawks would guide her and find projects that would be best suited to her and that would progress her career. It was the kind of prospect Betty couldn't turn down. A standard contract with one of the big studios guaranteed nothing; she would have been lost in the sea of pretty young girls who fought to be noticed, but if she was signed by Hawks, she had a chance to make it big.

• • •

The train journey took three days. Betty was on the brink of a new life, leaving behind her family and all she knew, heading towards a vast unknown. She was too much of a romantic dreamer to be scared; her dreams were big enough to overcome fear. This was certainly a turn of events she couldn't have predicted just months before, while she stalked agents and theatrical producers of Broadway, hoping for a walk-on, an understudy job, anything that would bring her one step closer to achieving her dream of a stage career. And now she was on her way to Hollywood, that distant place, synonymous with glamour and excitement, so far removed from all she knew that she never even dared to dream about it. She certainly didn't believe she had the physical attributes necessary for stardom. Garbo was a star. So was Rita Hayworth. Linda Darnell, Lana Turner, and Hedy Lamarr were the young, exquisite beauties currently making it big in the movies. They were all ultrafeminine, curvaceous, well-versed in the art of charm and seduction. Betty was different. Her success as a model did little to convince her that she was beautiful; she was simply young, fresh-faced, natural, and, above all, lucky. But even if that was all there was, she was not about to turn down her big chance. After all, Howard Hawks, the big Hollywood director, sent for her personally—and a man like that, with the best of the country's young talent at his disposal, must have had a good enough reason to go to all this trouble of sending for an unknown model he had only seen in a few photographs. Betty passed the time sipping ginger ales, pretending they were some exotic cocktails, practicing her most alluring poses in front of the mirror in her train compartment, carrying on elaborate conversations with the imagined figures of Feldman and Hawks. She was determined to impress them, to come across as sophisticated and worldly, to stash away the "nice Jewish girl from New York," and to present a vision of mystery she was convinced they'd want to see.

She arrived in Los Angeles on April 6, 1943, and was struck by just how different the city was from all she had known. The spring air was warm and balmy, palm trees lined the streets of white, single-story houses, all steeped in the California sun. There was a relaxed, laid-back feeling about the place; no one rushed around, there were no mad crowds. Betty was met at the station by Charlie Feldman's associate who drove her to the agent's office in Beverly Hills. The first meeting was brief but pleasant. "I liked him immediately," she would later recall. For his part, Feldman was relieved. He quickly assessed that the girl was striking, had a distinctive low voice, a good figure, and that despite being shy, she moved with confidence and grace. Moreover, she was intelligent and interesting, at once incredibly young and possessed of an air of maturity that far exceeded her years. He told her to go to her hotel, rest, and meet him for dinner later that evening. The next day, Betty wrote to her mother: "And don't tell this to anyone, but Charlie adores me. He thinks I'm wonderful, vital, alive, refreshing, full of fire, intelligent and few other things. And those, sweetie, are direct quotes." If Feldman was impressed by Betty, Hawks was slower to show his appreciation. He met the young model and Feldman for lunch the day after her arrival in Hollywood. To him, she looked like "just a kid." Nonetheless, he agreed that she had to be tested. It was to be a simple test, a single scene, and Feldman was to take care of the necessary preparations.

Feldman continued to be Betty's main protector and her guide into all things Hollywood. He invited Betty to his Beverly Hills home on the weekend after her arrival. Jean Howard, known for her keen eye and precise, if sometimes less than generous assessment of her husband's clients, told Charlie: "She just sounds like a tough kid to me. I think she's very pretty."

Initially, neither Feldman nor Hawks thought of Betty for *To Have and Have Not*. Her first screen test, in which she played a scene from *Claudia*, a play she had briefly understudied a year earlier in New York, was meant to determine her suitability for another picture, *Battle Cry*. The film, which Hawks was to direct for Warners before starting work on *To Have and Have Not*, was eventually abandoned by the studio. Feldman knew that the test would be crucial in showcasing Betty's potential, and by then Hawks was also beginning to see that the young girl had a special quality that he had failed to notice on their first meeting. Maybe, just maybe, she could be the great star he had always longed to discover.

Hawks decided to not only direct the test, but to personally oversee every aspect of it, and make sure that Betty was given the best possible opportunity to shine. Slim, who met her discovery some days after Betty arrived in Los Angeles, was also convinced that her initial instinct was correct. She was only a few years older than Betty, but she possessed the kind of style and sophistication Betty longed for, and she quickly became a close friend and a role model. Betty spent the night before the test at the Feldmans, where Charlie and Jean did their best to relax her and make her feel that she was "among friends." The prospect of testing before the camera, and before Hawks, was terrifying. Will she prove a huge disappointment to these people who put so much trust in her and who had shown her so much kindness? Was her career going to be over before it ever began? She didn't seem able to control her nerves, she shook violently and threw up, before finally falling into a deep, exhausted sleep, the kind only the very young are afforded.

The test was a success. The camera not only captured Betty's fresh beauty; it also magnified the intriguing, mysterious quality Slim Hawks had noticed in the *Harper's* photos. She was more than just photogenic; she had undeniable charisma and screen presence. Yes, she was the real deal. A contract was quickly drawn up, and on May 3, 1943, Betty Bacall signed it, becoming the personal property of Howard Hawks. Her salary was $100 a week, with an option to go up to $1,500 a week, should she prove a success. Betty was overcome with happiness; she couldn't have dreamed for a better turn of events. She was now able to invite her mother to come over to California, where they would share an apartment on 275 South Reeves Drive, her first Hollywood address.

Their reunion was joyous and emotional, and after weeks of relaying the excitement through letters, Betty could finally tell Natalie everything in person. Their bond was as close as ever, and it would always remain so, but the weeks in Hollywood had installed a new independence in Betty. She knew she was able to stand on her own feet, to take control of her life. She was now a young woman, a professional actress, earning a steady salary and learning her trade.

• • •

The weeks following the screen test were spent learning, practicing, reading aloud to train her voice, and waiting. Betty soon learned that waiting was an inextricable part of being an actor. She phoned Feldman's office daily—was there any word from Howard? When would she be working? She was frantic, gazing into the mirror at her eighteen-year-old face in search of wrinkles—if she had to wait much longer, her time would no doubt pass. Feldman continuously and patiently assured her that when the time was right, she would be working.

Betty also applied for a driver's license. From the very first day of her arrival, she was made painfully aware that, unlike in New York, in California, the inability to drive severely limited her movements. Having to rely on other people to drive her around felt constraining, and so Betty spent the spring months of 1943 taking driving lessons, and after passing her test in June bought her first car, a 1940 Plymouth coupe. Knowing how much emphasis Hawks had put on the importance of voice, she would drive to a secluded spot up on Mulholland Drive, and spent hours reading aloud, trying to keep her voice low no matter what emotion she was expressing. While her voice was naturally low and husky, Hawks noted that when excited, she tended to get more high-pitched, which, in his mind, ruined many otherwise perfect movie scenes. After weeks of practice, Betty decided to showcase her new and improved projection to Hawks. She arrived at his office, and as Hawks later remembered, "she talked way down, you know. She'd changed her voice. And—what the hell, you *have* to notice a girl like that."

By the end of the summer, Hawks was becoming more and more convinced that Betty could be right for *To Have and Have Not*. There was another major female role in the film, one that Warners insisted was cast with one of their contract players. If things didn't work out during production, if Bacall proved too inexperienced to pull off the performance, the balance could be shifted to give the other girl more scenes. It was more than slightly risky to entrust such a vital role to a total newcomer, but Hawks was a gambler. He knew Betty was nervous before the camera, but as her screen test had already shown, when the camera was rolling, something magical happened. If he could guide her through the film as carefully as he had through the test, she surely could recreate that magic. By now *Battle Cry* had been abandoned by Warners, and Hawks had the green light to focus solely on *To Have and Have Not*. To test Betty's reaction, Hawks said to her one day: "I want to put you in a movie with either Cary Grant or Humphrey Bogart." Betty's reaction was, "Cary Grant—terrific! Humphrey Bogart—yuck."

By 1943, Humphrey Bogart was not only Warners' biggest male star, but perhaps the biggest name in the business. *Casablanca*, released earlier that year, elevated his status from a reliable leading man to an iconic screen hero. His blend of cynicism and heroism perfectly reflected the mood of the era, making Bogart the emblematic figure of the perfect wartime American: tough and cool, no-nonsense on the surface but essentially a closeted, romantic idealist. In the winter of 1943, Bogart was busy filming *Passage to Marseille*, a costly and conflict-ridden production designed to capitalize on the success of *Casablanca*, reuniting much of the film's cast, again under the direction of Michael Curtiz. It was during the festive season, as filming was drawing to a close, that Bogart received a visit from Howard Hawks. Hawks was set to direct Bogart's next movie, and the actor was happy to see him; he couldn't wait to put *Passage to Marseille* behind him and focus on the new project. The cast was still in the process of being assembled, and the female lead was yet to be found. Hawks, with an enigmatic smile, told Bogart: "Come with me. I want you to meet somebody." Behind the huge lights that were being set up for the next scene, on a wooden bench, sat a young woman. She stood up, and Hawks introduced them: "Bogie, this is Betty Bacall." "There was no clap of thunder, no lightning bolt," Bacall would later write. She thought him slight and unimpressive, and he too thought little of the encounter. She was certainly a pretty young thing, but this was Hollywood—there was no wartime rationing on beauty. But even if the sparks didn't instantly fly between the two, there was enough electricity in the air for Hawks's skilled eye to recognize the potential. As a Christmas present that year, Hawks offered Betty the good tidings: she would test for the role in *To Have and Have Not*.

She was ecstatic and terrified in equal measures. This was a major chance for a big break, a role in a film opposite one of the biggest stars in Hollywood. It wasn't quite clear just how big of a role it was going to be; all she had to work with was a single scene. Charlie Feldman told her that the chance of getting the part "was good—that Howard would not be making the test if he didn't think so too." For the next couple of weeks, Betty would drive over to Hawks's office to rehearse. It was the scene that would eventually become iconic, the sexually charged, innuendo-infused "you know how to whistle" encounter between Steve and Slim (nicknames the characters give one another in the film). For Betty, whose inexperience as an actress was matched by her sexual innocence, rehearsing the scene often left her feeling embarrassed and uneasy. Sexuality is Slim's most reliable weapon, her only tool of survival. It is her sexual confidence, combined with vulnerability and the need for protection that constitutes the heart of the scene. The actress who portrays her needs to possess a strong enough presence to carry out a seduction, but even more than that, to initiate the relationship, to demand it—a task usually reserved for male characters. John Ridgely, a veteran character actor, who often appeared in Warners' gangster films, and who would one day work with Bogart and Bacall in *The Big Sleep*, played Steve to Betty's Slim in rehearsals as well as in the actual test.

They finally shot it. Bacall delivered the famous line on film for the first time. "You know how to whistle, don't you, Steve? You just put your lips together and blow." She couldn't have known that the line would haunt her for the rest of her life, that decades from that moment journalists would ask her to quote it, that it would take on a life of its own, removed from the narrative of the film. All she knew was that it was over, that Hawks seemed pleased, as did Charlie Feldman, and apparently, Jack Warner. After what seemed like forever, Hawks finally broke the news to her: she had the part. He also told her that from now on her name was Lauren Bacall.

By this point, the press had already caught wind of the new star-to-be. "She's a secret," reported one Hollywood columnist. "Last time we saw her, she had no name—yet. She is now Lauren Bacall." The item continued to state that Hawks's discovery was "definitely worth writing about": "Tall, slim, long-legged, tawny-gold hair, blue-green eyes in a chiseled, interesting face—a sort of Katharine Hepburn with curves. Something electric about her, and smoldering." This was exactly the sort of publicity Hawks had hoped for. All the Hollywood columnists wanted to meet her, to write about her. Hawks made sure she wasn't overexposed, that the balance between keeping them interested and maintaining an air of mystery about her was in place. Lauren Bacall was the perfect product of the producer's imagination. Her new name reflected the glamour and worldliness she was expected to project. She would never be fully at ease with the name or the image. Her friends and family would go on calling her Betty for the rest of her life. To the public though, she would be Lauren Bacall.

Aside from her name, the other, perhaps more serious problem weighing on her mind was her Jewish identity. Even during her early modeling days in New York, she had been made aware of her "otherness," that her ethnic background and familial religious tradition somewhat set her apart from others in the business. Now, in Hollywood, where the main studios were largely run by Jews, she suddenly became more self-conscious than ever before. During those first few months, Hawks had made a number of antisemitic remarks in her presence, making her feel deeply uncomfortable and worried, and completely paralyzed at the thought of standing up to him. Should he ever find out about her heritage, would he fire her? She hated herself for feeling this way, not knowing that she was in no way alone in her predicament. This was 1943—at the very same time, in Europe, in the very same lands where her family had come from, her people were being rounded up into ghettos, imprisoned in Nazi concentration camps, and gassed to death. While the US was certainly a safe haven by comparison, here too antisemitism was widespread. The standards of female beauty promoted by movie magazines and by movies themselves were based on pretty much the same Arian model on which the Nazis based their policies of ethnic purism. A certain degree of exoticism was permitted, but the few leading ladies with a Jewish background were actively encouraged to conceal their true ethnic identity. With her light coloring and Slavic features, Bacall didn't fit the stereotypical image of what was perceived as "Jewish." This made her all the more uncomfortable whenever someone expressed their shock and disbelief at finding out "the truth." It would be many years before she'd find the courage to speak frankly of her own Jewishness. Bacall wasn't alone in playing this duplicitous game. Others, including Hedy Lamarr, Luise Rainer, and the English actress Claire Bloom all had successful careers during the classical Hollywood era, but none talked openly about their Jewish heritage during those years.

• • •

The cameras on *To Have and Have Not* started rolling on February 29, 1944, on the Warners backlot in Burbank—over the Hollywood Hills, a few miles east of Beverly Hills. There was a sense of busy excitement in the air, the first day of making a new movie. The newly named Lauren Bacall arrived promptly at 9 a.m., although she wasn't to begin shooting her first scene until the following day—she was there to learn, to meet the crew, to observe. No one seemed worried by the fact that the script was still far from complete. To the contrary, the sense of unknown only aroused Hawks's enthusiasm. Bogart's wife, Mayo Methot, came to the set on the first day. Her marriage to Bogie had by that time become notorious in Hollywood—she was an alcoholic, known for her drunken and often violent rages. Lauren was introduced to Methot, unaware of the storm that was brewing on the horizon. She was too busy worrying about her first appearance in the movie to see Bogart as anything other than her costar: an experienced, celebrated actor, who could either lift her up or shatter her already fragile self-esteem. On the second day, it became apparent that he was there to support and guide her, to make sure that she was as good as she could possibly be. She was to learn that this was the trait of all great actors; supporting your costars is as important as focusing on your own performance.

The first scene they shot was also Slim's introduction to Steve and her first appearance in the film. "Anybody got a match?" It was an entrance designed to impress—not only Bogart's character in the film but also the audience, who would lay eyes on Lauren Bacall for the first time. Watching the scene today, it's impossible to detect the nervousness, the awesome burden of expectation the young actress is carrying on her shoulders. Such is the magic of the movies, the skill of the director, the care of the costar, and, perhaps most importantly, the natural, undefinable quality of a star. In reality, Lauren was overcome with anxiety, trembling violently when Hawks called action. The first take was a disaster: her hand shook so badly that she struggled to light her cigarette. Bogart, a veteran of over fifty films and countless stage plays, looked at his young costar with admiration. He saw just how nervous she was, and he joked around to relax her. "I found out very quickly that first day what a terrific man Bogart was," Lauren would write decades later. "He did everything possible to put me at ease. He was on my side." As the day went on, Lauren realized that the one way to stop her head from trembling was to lower her chin and look up. It worked, and the camera loved it—it was exactly the kind of enigmatic, provocative gaze the character required, and the studio publicity would later dub it "The Look," another piece of the film's legacy which was to become a permanent element of Lauren Bacall's star image.

From that day, the shoot went smoothly. Under Hawks's skilled direction, Bacall was creating a mysterious, multidimensional character, and her onscreen presence was magnetic. Her inexperience did show but rather than hindering her performance, it seemed to add to her appeal. She also got to sing, something she was unsure she could do. Contrary to the Hollywood legend, the voice heard in the movie is not that of Andy Williams—although Hawks did ask the singer the record the vocals in case some of the high notes had to be dubbed But in the end, he decided to only use Bacall's original recording. Betty's sultry performance of "How Little We Know" became one of the highlights of the film.

It was clear that Bogart had taken Lauren under his wing. He became her champion and protector, as well as teacher. It was platonic, at first. Their love began on film before it spilled into real life, the dailies unmistakably showing that their chemistry was magical. Dolores Moran, a young contract player for whom Warners had high hopes, played the second female lead, but as the shoot and the daily rewriting of the script progressed, her part became smaller, while Hawks placed all his energy on building the picture around Bogart and Bacall. He ought to have been more than pleased—his instincts proved accurate: Lauren Bacall was on her way to becoming the star he had always dreamed of creating. But his contentment was marred by his jealousy of Lauren's growing closeness to Bogie—it was becoming apparent that she was going to be a great success, but as Bogart's costar rather than as Hawks's discovery.

Gradually, some weeks into the filming, the cast and crew started to accept Bogie and Bacall as something of an item, although at first no one took it seriously. In the first place, there was a twenty-five-year age gap between them. Bogart was married, for the third time no less, and to a mentally unstable, violently possessive woman. Bacall was young and inexperienced. It was seen as part of the Hollywood game—young women were expected to have sexual relationships with older, influential men in order to advance their careers. The question of unequal power dynamics wasn't part of the discourse. Lauren would later reflect that Hawks had his own designs on his young protégé, and that he was furious that Bogart came along before he could make his move. Everyone, including Natalie and Hawks, warned her against getting involved with Bogie. "When the picture is over Bogart will forget all about you. That's the last you'll ever see of him," Hawks told her. Her mother echoed his thoughts: "What kind of man is that—with a wife—who'd be seeing a girl twenty-five years younger?"

But to Bogart this was something else. He knew the Hollywood scene well: the affairs, the casting couch, the infidelities. In all his years in Hollywood, he had never had an affair with one of his costars. At forty-five, he had all but abandoned the hopes of a happy marriage or a family—perhaps it just wasn't in the stars for him. Betty Bacall (he would always call her "Betty," or "Baby") was unlike anyone he had known before. For all her innocence and youth, she had an emotional maturity and strength of character which astounded him. She was certainly no immature starlet looking for thrills or publicity—the intensity of his feelings towards her stopped him in his tracks. He wanted to protect her, to be with her, to give himself another chance at happiness. And she wanted it too: "My falling in love had definitely taken over and put the biggest, most exciting thing that ever happened in my work life into second place," Lauren reflected decades later. Bogart certainly represented the protective, fatherlike figure that had been missing from her life ever since her own father had left. He was also the best kind of Hollywood mentor a young actress could wish for. Just how much the young Bacall was aware of all those factors isn't clear. In later years, she would always resent any suggestions that Bogie had been a father figure or, indeed, that her involvement with him had anything to do with career ambitions.

The shooting of *To Have and Have Not* finished on May 10, 1944. They shot some publicity stills, sultry poses of the two lovers wrapped in each other's arms. Hawks, happy with his movie and convinced that the affair between Bogie and Bacall would be over along with filming, now focused on editing the material. Lauren left the studio alone, driving back to Beverly Hills, to the apartment she shared with her mother.

CHAPTER 3

Bogie and Bacall

"VOLUMES HAVE BEEN WRITTEN IN THE ATTEMPT TO EXPLAIN THE ILLUSIVE quality that made Cleopatra appeal to Julius Caesar or that marked Theda Bara as an early screen menace. But the fact remains that it is something a woman is or isn't, has or hasn't—something that words seem to be inadequate to describe, but which every human being recognizes at once. Miss Bacall, by unanimous opinion of previewers, certainly has it."

The above item is one of countless pieces that appeared in the wake of *To Have and Have Not* opening in New York City on October 11, 1944, all filled with praise for the nineteen-year-old, who had suddenly been catapulted to stardom. "Lauren Bacall has cinema personality to burn," announced *Time*, raving about her "stone-crushing self-confidence" and "trombone voice." *Life* called her "one of the great movie discoveries of all time," choosing her picture to grace their October 1944 cover.

The film itself was a hit, even if reviewers were divided. Warners decided to roll it out slowly, build up the good word of mouth, and gradually open the movie to a wider audience. By the end of the year, *To Have and Have Not* would become one of the top ten box-office hits of 1944, and its popularity continued into 1945.

Lauren Bacall was a sensation. One writer predicted the imminent birth of a "Bacall Cult," based solely on her single film appearance. For all the carefully designed promotional campaigns, calculated moves, and publicity gimmicks Hollywood studios had engaged in from the very beginning of their existence, the final word on who reaches stardom had always belonged to the audience. Howard Hawks knew he had found someone special in Bacall. Warners had high hopes for her too, but ultimately, the rapturous public response to her was a surprise to all concerned. No one could have predicted it. The papers compared her to the screen deities who had come before: Hepburn, Davis, Garbo, West, Dietrich. And while she evoked elements of all of them, what made Bacall an instant star was precisely the fact that there had been no one like her before. Her look, her insolence, her style, were uniquely hers—she was a woman perfectly in alignment with the mood of her time. Onscreen, she appeared independent, confident, aware of the power of her sexuality, unashamed to use her allure to her own advantage, without apologizing for it. Yet she was not a femme fatale. She wasn't out to destroy a man. She simply existed; all she asked for was the right to be—she could be loved, but she couldn't be possessed. She made her own choices. If Bogie embodied the wartime American male, she was more than adequate as his female counterpart.

Most of the legendary stars she was compared to had spent years crafting their images, aided by directors, makeup people, photographers, studio heads, publicity departments. Trial and error, trying out different parts, leading men, slowly finding out what worked for them. Bacall wouldn't have the luxury of preparing for and easing into fame. Her star persona was fully formed with her very first film. Over subsequent decades, she would try to reshape it, often against tough odds and with varying success, but the figure of the sultry siren, drenched in shadows, leaning over Humphrey Bogart, giving his unshaven face a light slap, telling him to whistle if he needed her—that's cinema at its most magical and most seductive, a star image that endures.

From the start, the public loved Bogie and Bacall together. Their onscreen pairing generated heat; their chemistry was undeniable. Howard Hawks might have been less than pleased about it. Bacall was, to his mind, his girl, his discovery. Instead, she was now undeniably associated with Bogart. Warner Bros., which owned half of Lauren's contract, was delighted with the winning combination. It had never been planned, it just happened, and suddenly the studio found themselves in possession of the hottest double act in Hollywood. With their first feature still earning big bucks across the country, the studio quickly arranged for a follow-up.

The Big Sleep had been planned as a vehicle for Bogart even before *To Have and Have Not* came out, but with the sudden Bacall-mania taking over America, the film had to be reimagined as an opportunity to showcase Bogie and Bacall together again. Based on a novel by Raymond Chandler, the film would over the years become known as one of the best examples of the noir genre—if not entirely for its visual style, certainly for its convoluted plot, shady characters, and the clever use of dialogue. Bogart plays Philip Marlowe, a cynical, wisecracking private eye, with Lauren as Vivian, the eldest daughter of a wealthy general. Both get mixed up in a murder mystery, and naturally, fall in love in the process. Along the way, there's gambling, pornography, all manner of intrigue—all cleverly veiled from the censors by way of euphemism and double entendre.

The production started in October 1944, just as *To Have and Have Not* was being released. It was a reunion for Lauren and Bogie, both on camera and off, as they had spent the months following the end of their first movie largely apart, with a few discreet meetings. Bogie was riddled with guilt about the end of his marriage. He knew it was over, Mayo Methot knew it too, but she still clung to her husband, and he had very real concerns about her mental state. They finally announced their separation that fall, just a week after cameras on *The Big Sleep* started rolling.

For Lauren, the previous six months had been an emotional rollercoaster—she had fallen in love with a married man, who also happened to be a famous movie star, twenty-five years her senior. She herself became a star, almost overnight, and had to deal with all the pressures that came with it, totally unprepared. How does one prepare for fame? There is no crash course for it—even if there had been, there was no one to offer it to her. In September of that year, just weeks before her first motion picture premiered in New York, Lauren's beloved grandmother Sophie died. It was a huge blow—that vital link to her family's past, a source of love, even if sometimes of the tough sort, was gone forever.

While most of the cast and crew working on *The Big Sleep* accepted the fact that Lauren and Bogie were an item, it was by no means an easy time for the two. The press sensed a story—and it was a big one: a case of cinematic magic crossing over into reality. For the moment, the public was kept in the dark about the romance—after all, Bogart was still a married man—but the Hollywood columnists were well aware of the situation. Hedda Hopper, the queen of the gossip columns, delighted in being in on the scoop, even offering advice to the young star. "Beware of Mayo Methot, dear," she warned Bacall. "She will drop one of the hot lamps on your head. She'll stop at nothing." The pressure was overwhelming. At the same time, Lauren was busy making a difficult movie, only her second, still very much learning each step of the way. She also had to deal with the uncertainty and emotional upheaval of her first love, under circumstances that were less than ideal. During the course of filming, Bogie continued to be torn between his feelings for Lauren and the sense of obligation he felt towards Methot. He was drinking again, and for the first time, his drinking interfered with his professionalism. He'd arrive on the set late, often in no condition to go before the camera. Some days, he wouldn't show up at all. He went back to his estranged wife, before once again separating that December. "We had some bumpy rides," Lauren would remember decades later. "He left his wife, he went back to his wife—I just thought, you have to face it, it's finished." As weeks went by, it was clear to both they just couldn't face being apart. Questioned by Louella Parsons, Hopper's archrival for the gossip queen crown, Bogie said, "I have told Mayo I am not coming home. She can have anything she wants if she will let me go. I believe she is too sensible to want to hold me after six years of continual battling." The Bogart-Methot marriage was over, with their divorce finalized in May of the following year, just as the world celebrated the end of World War II.

In the middle of all the personal drama, an exceptional film was being made. All the creative forces that came together on *The Big Sleep* aligned to make a near-perfect film noir. Hawks was once again directing, and regardless of his personal feelings about the romance between the two stars, he was able to capture their electrifying chemistry, perhaps even more effectively than the first time around. The screenplay, again penned by William Faulkner, with additional scenes written by Leigh Breckett and Jules Furthman, didn't have a clear structure, with rewrites taking place daily. Some days, Hawks and his actors were themselves confused by the multiple plot twists. What kept the production going was the film's cast, Faulkner's brilliant dialogue, and Hawks's ability to hold it all together.

For Lauren, having Hawks's guidance remained invaluable. She trusted him, knowing he'd get the best out of her. The character of Vivian is more complex than Slim. Vivian had been married and divorced, enjoys gambling, and feels comfortable in the shady, male-populated underworld. At the same time, she is a sophisticated and elegant socialite, a woman with a sharp tongue and a quick answer for everything. Her sexuality is confident and unabashed; she's equally skilled at seducing and scolding Marlowe. Vivian is perhaps the closest Bacall ever got to playing an actual femme fatale. While she's not out to destroy Marlowe, she has the power to, and throughout the film, her intentions are never certain. She is a dangerous woman, and Bacall embodies her elusiveness brilliantly. There are still moments in the film where Lauren's inexperience shows—at times, she tends to resort to posing, modellike, instead of throwing herself authentically into a scene. But she's also able to hold her own in her scenes with Bogie, effortlessly handling Faulkner's dialogue, injecting comedy and pathos with equal effectiveness. She also gets to sing, performing "And Her Tears Flowed Like Wine," a quirky song that underscores the movie's dark sense of humor.

While Bogie rarely offered her acting advice, it was through observing him at work that Lauren learned. Acting was about instinct and intention—there was thought behind every action. In one scene, she was required to enter a room and walk over to the door. After the first take, while the camera was being reset, Bogie took her aside. "Where are you coming from? What were you doing in the other room?" he asked. "You were doing something, think about that. Don't just walk in like a model." It was a lesson she'd never forget. "I learned to prepare from Bogie, I learned to think before the scene started," Lauren reflected in 1995. "What I'd just been doing, what had just happened, who I had been talking with. What the situation was. Not to just start talking with an empty head when the director said 'action.'"

Bacall was not the only woman in the cast—in fact, *The Big Sleep* is one of the most female-driven noirs ever made. Bogart finds himself surrounded by women throughout the picture, all instantly attracted to him, willing to aid his investigation. From the bookstore proprietress, memorably played by Dorothy Malone, to the female taxi driver, the cloakroom attendant, and the unstable Carmen—Vivian's younger sister, played by Martha Vickers—the women of *The Big Sleep* are the collective driving force behind the film's narrative. There is space in the movie for all of them, although it is Bacall's Vivian who walks away with Marlowe at the end. The original cut of the movie left Charlie Feldman feeling that not enough emphasis was placed on Bacall and that Hawks hadn't shot enough scenes between her and Bogie. She was meant to be the star, not just one more actress in the female ensemble. It's possible that Hawks intentionally shifted the balance of the movie away from Lauren as a way to punish her for her affair with Bogie. For the time being, the studio kept the film on hold, busy releasing the last of their wartime efforts before they became irrelevant. In January 1946, a year after filming wrapped, Jack Warner ordered additional scenes to be shot, with some of the existing sequences reshot. Hawks agreed, and the three of them—Hawks, Bogie, and Bacall—would work their magic one last time. The now iconic scene of Bogie and Bacall in a restaurant, trading barely concealed sexual innuendos, was one of those added during that time. She looked more beautiful than ever; the costumes designed for her by Leah Rhodes highlighted her mysterious allure to perfection. *The Big Sleep* would show off Bacall at her most glamorous, the epitome of a film noir heroine. Along with Rita Hayworth's *Gilda* and

Ava Gardner's Kitty Collins in *The Killers*—both movies also released in 1946—Bacall captured the public's imagination at a very particular moment, just as the war had ended. Men were returning home to find their women changed. They were now independent, sexually liberated, a danger to the ancient patriarchal order. Yet, underneath the tough exterior, the cinematic women were still vulnerable, still waiting for their knights. In the end, Gilda walks away with Glenn Ford. Kitty Collins, despite her duplicitous ways, only longs for a home and a husband. Vivian, too, wants to be loved, and she's not afraid to ask Marlowe to love her. In the end, to the delight of the moviegoing public, Bogie and Bacall live happily ever after. Somewhere along the way, the line between life and cinematic fiction was forever blurred.

• • •

They were married on May 21, 1945, just days after Bogie's divorce was finalized. The ceremony took place at the home of Bogie's friend, Louis Bromfield, at the Malabar Farm in Ohio. It was meant to be a simple affair—no Hollywood guests, no glitzy reception, just a celebration of their love. Unfortunately, the press was tipped off, and on the morning of the wedding swarms of reporters tried to force their way onto the property. Lauren remained calm—it was her day, hers and Bogie's, and nothing else mattered. She was dressed in a simple pink suit, with a corsage of orchids. She looked pale and gorgeous, very much in love. In the absence of the studio lights and makeup, her youth and innocence were striking. Bogie was emotional—it was the fourth time lucky for him, and he really believed that this time it would be lucky. During the short ceremony, Bogie cried—he had always cried at weddings—"He's very cute about it," Lauren later joked. Natalie was the sole representative of Lauren's family, doing double duty as mother of the bride and matron of honor. She had recently gotten married herself and was now Mrs. Lee Goldberg. Few friends were in attendance—gifts and telegrams had been sent to the newlyweds' new home at King's Road in the Hollywood Hills. Jack Warner presented Lauren with a Buick convertible, both as a wedding gift and a bonus acknowledging her recent success.

Marrying Bogie meant that Lauren automatically became part of the Hollywood elite, even if Bogie himself was a reluctant member of it. Less than a year after her debut, with only one released picture to her credit, Lauren Bacall was one of the biggest movie stars in the world. Howard Hawks, his ego wounded by what he saw as Lauren's betrayal, washed his hands of his discovery. After *The Big Sleep*, he sold his share of Bacall's contract to Warner Bros. She was left without his guidance and nurturing, and she would soon find out that the studio had little idea of how to handle her. Wanting to capitalize on her popularity and the publicity generated by her marriage to Bogie, Jack Warner cast Lauren as a lead in the adaptation of Graham Greene's novel, *The Confidential Agent*, which started shooting the week after the wedding. With their new home still not ready, the Bogarts set up at the Garden of Allah, and they both returned to work—for the first time, Lauren would be working on a film without the support of either Bogie or Hawks.

She knew she wasn't right for the part, which called for her to play an upper-class English heiress. No dialect coach had been hired to help her achieve even a semblance of a British accent. The film's director, Herman Shumlin, offered her little help. Charles Boyer was cast as her leading man, clearly indicating that the studio hoped to replicate the successful formula of the Bogart-Bacall pairing by teaming Lauren up with another well-established and much older actor. This time, however, the chemistry was not there. In the movie, Boyer, who was less than six months older than Bogie, looks more like a paternal figure than a romantic hero, while Lauren, without Hawks's glamorous framing, appears even younger than her twenty-one years. Her nerves and inexperience are apparent, although her performance isn't entirely bad—there are moments when she's effective and touching, showcasing a great deal of raw potential brewing under the surface, waiting to be extracted.

With *Big Sleep* still on hold, the studio rushed *Confidential Agent* into release in the fall of 1945, hoping to cash in on the buzz that still surrounded the Bogarts' recent nuptials. Jack Warner thought her performance to be strong. Sadly, the critics disagreed. Just as she'd been unprepared for the overwhelming amount of praise she'd received after *To Have and Have Not*, the negative press which followed the opening of *Confidential Agent* was something Lauren was unequipped to deal with.

"From the moment Lauren Bacall appears on the screen—a full head taller than Boyer—and announces in a nasal American voice that she is the daughter of an English lord, she is outplayed, even by the musical background," wrote one critic. In later years, Lauren would look back on the film as the greatest disaster of her career.

"If I had had the care from Hawks, that I might have had if he wasn't such a macho man, furious that I went off with Bogie, that movie never would have happened," she reflected decades later. "The fact is that it hurt me a lot. [It went from] all the critics that had praised me, that had said I was the combination of Garbo and Hepburn and Dietrich, that I was this most exciting, brilliant, wonderful, funny—every compliment in the book—to, we were wrong! Send her back where she came from! It was very hurtful."

What helped to soften the blow was her relationship with Bogart. They were now happily married, the two of them against the world. She was "Baby," a nickname he liked to use for her, and one the press gladly picked up, forever after referring to Bacall as "Bogie's Baby." Bogart had known both the greatest heights of success and the crushing lows of critical failure. His attitude, which Lauren also assumed, was to not take any of it too seriously—if you believe the good reviews, you'll have to also believe the bad ones. It was best to take it all with a grain of salt.

The failure of *Confidential Agent* made Lauren distrustful of Jack Warner and the offers he would send her—in the coming years, she would turn down a great number of scripts, refusing to do anything which she felt wasn't right for her. She also focused her attention on being Mrs. Humphrey Bogart. She was still ambitious and wanted to prove herself a good actress, but Bogie came first. She had promised him never to go away on location, and to accompany him on his. The arrangement might not have been entirely fair to her, but she insisted that she was happy with it. "We had made a pact that I would always put marriage first, and I did," she said in 1995. "My career meant everything to me, and yet Bogie meant more, and I certainly am not sorry I lived up to our pact." There were certainly things to work on, adjustments to be made. During the first months following the wedding, Bogie found it hard to leave his old ways behind. He still drank a lot, a pattern fueled by the feelings of guilt about leaving Mayo Method. Some nights he'd go out on the town with his Hollywood buddies, leaving his young wife alone in their big home. Sometimes she would join him, but nights of boozing would never become her thing. Gradually, Bogie found peace. Lauren's levelheaded attitude and the genuine, youthful love she offered him helped to lay his demons to rest. He'd swap nightly escapades for quiet evenings at home in the company of a few close friends. The future was looking bright.

The Big Sleep was finally released in the late summer of 1946, becoming a smash hit, with critics loving Bacall once again, if more cautiously than the first time around. The reshoots and additional scenes which had been filmed earlier that year made the picture even more decisively a Bogart-Bacall vehicle, solidifying their status as the number one Hollywood couple, onscreen and off. The film's success would lead to two further pictures together. The first, *Dark Passage*, went into production a few weeks after the premiere of *The Big Sleep*. The Bogarts traveled to San Francisco for a month of location shooting. It was to be a happy experience. The film was a unique take on the noir genre, with the writer/director Delmer Daves utilizing a number of innovative narrative and visual devices to tell his story. Lauren had a strong part, significantly different from her previous noir incarnations. Because the first half of the film is told from Bogie's subjective point of view—his face doesn't appear onscreen until after his character undergoes plastic surgery—Bacall is allowed to shine, especially as seen through his eyes, and she fully takes advantage of the opportunity. She's softer than ever before, allowed to showcase her caring, maternal side, while also maintaining her mystery. Daves's close-ups of her are among the most memorable of her career—he's interested in showcasing more than only her beauty; his camera captures all the nuance and mystery than makes her such an irresistible screen presence.

The film's San Francisco setting, and the studio's decision to actually shoot on location rather than on the Burbank backlot, added to the movie's texture, helping to make *Dark Passage* the most visually thrilling entry in the Bogie-Bacall catalogue. The film premiered in September of 1947 and became another hit with audiences. Critics were mostly generous, and this time, it was Lauren's acting that stole the show. The all-powerful Bosley Crowther of the *New York Times* was underwhelmed by Bogie's turn, but liked Bacall, stating that "the mood of [Bogart's] performance is compensated somewhat by that of Miss Bacall, who generates quite a lot of pressure as a sharp-eyed, knows-what-she-wants girl."

Lauren's success in *The Big Sleep* and *Dark Passage* ought to have led to more juicy parts and interesting projects, but Jack Warner still had little idea of what to do with the young star, beyond pairing her with Bogart. Together, the Bogarts guaranteed strong box-office returns, and it was the bottom line that most interested Warner. By this point, Bogie was the highest paid actor in Hollywood, with Hedda Hopper reporting him to have "one of the best contracts" of any studio star. Following *Dark Passage*, he would go on to appear in John Huston's *The Treasure of the Sierra Madre*, widely considered to be one of his best performances.

For Lauren, her next film would be *Key Largo*, again opposite Bogie, in their last big screen pairing. The film was also directed by Huston, Bogie's close friend and favorite director, who was also to subsequently become an important figure in Bacall's life.

Unlike *Dark Passage*, *Key Largo* wouldn't have the advantage of a location shoot, with principal photography taking place at Warners' backlot. But the combination of Huston's direction and the brilliant ensemble of actors, which included Edward G. Robinson, Lionel Barrymore, and Claire Trevor, more than made up for the modest budget. For Lauren, working with Huston was a significant change from her previous experiences with directors. He respected her input, encouraged her to improvise and contribute ideas, and promoted a more laid-back atmosphere on the set. "John was wonderful with actors," she later remembered. "He never embarrassed you, never gave you direction in front of other people. He'd always put his arm around you and walk you over to the side, and the atmosphere on the set was always very professional, but friendly. He was much easier to communicate with than Hawks."

Lauren didn't think much of her part in the film. Her character—a young war widow, living with her late husband's invalid father in a small, coastal hotel—doesn't get the big, showy scenes. In the end, it was Claire Trevor who won the best supporting actress Oscar for her turn as the alcoholic gangster's moll, and yet, Bacall's restrained performance is effective. Huston captures the subtle shades of sadness, of hope, of rage, all of which Bacall is able to communicate without much dialogue. The by-then legendary chemistry between Bogie and Bacall is tangible in the movie, though as captured by Huston, they appear softer, their bond extending beyond sexual tension and clever double entendres. They glance at each other with genuine love, the camera capturing their deep affection for one another more fully than in any other film. Huston also uses the film as an opportunity to inject thinly veiled political commentary. In one scene Bacall implores Bogart to act on his moral convictions: "Maybe it is a rotten world. But a cause isn't lost as long there's someone willing to go on fighting."

Considering Huston, Bogart, and Bacall's political involvement at the time, these lines carry less-than-subtle messages about protecting the freedom of expression which they felt was being threatened.

Once again, the film did well at the box office and was well received by critics, yet, curiously, there would be no more Bogie-Bacall movies. It's interesting to consider why the studio failed to further capitalize on their most reliable acting duo's power to draw in crowds. Bogie's desire to develop his own production company, Santana Productions, led him in a different creative direction—the ultimate failure of the enterprise would be a source of great disappointment to him. His wife's professional ambitions didn't seem to be at the forefront of his mind—in any case, he never interfered in her career or lobbied for her to be cast in a picture. Another reason was closer to home: Lauren was determined to give Bogie the loving family life he'd never known, which meant children. Bogie felt unsure about becoming a father for the first time at this stage of his life, but he'd come to fully embrace the role. Their son, whom they'd name Stephen Humphrey Bogart, was born on January 6, 1949, less than a year before Bogie's fiftieth birthday. A daughter, Leslie Howard Bogart (named in honor of Bogie's great friend, the British actor Leslie Howard), followed on August 23, 1952. The Bogarts moved from Benedict Canyon to a large mansion in Holmby Hills—their new home would come to symbolize the close-knit community of friends, who just happened to be some of the most illustrious figures in the world of entertainment. Bogie also fulfilled his lifelong dream of owning a sailboat. The Santana would become his refuge, the symbol of his independence. Lauren didn't share Bogie's love of sailing, although she'd spend many weekends on the boat with him. She threw herself into the role of a wife and mother, a friend and a hostess, while also expanding her interest in art and politics.

The Bogarts' politics would sometimes land them in hot water. Back in the fall of 1947, just as *Dark Passage* was playing to packed houses around the country, Hollywood was shaken by the first concentrated effort of the House Un-American Activities Committee to expose and blacklist filmdom's liberal elites. After ten writers and directors, "the Hollywood Ten," were subpoenaed to appear before the committee to testify and inform on the political affiliations of their friends and colleagues, both Lauren and Bogie were outraged. They weren't the only ones—most of their friends could talk of nothing else. Soon, the Committee for the First Amendment was established, with Bacall, Bogart, and Gene Kelly among its founding members. Stars including Katharine Hepburn, Ava Gardner, Henry Fonda, and Gregory Peck would also add their signatures to the committee's statement.

In October, they flew to Washington, DC. Along with the Bogarts, the group included John Huston, Ira Gershwin, John Garfield, Danny Kaye, Evelyn Keyes, and others. Naturally, the press had a field day. Images of the group, with the unmistakable figures of Bogie and Bacall at the forefront, were printed in newspapers around the country. As they were soon to find out, any association with communism, real or imagined, had the potential to ruin a career with one smooth sweep. "This has nothing to do with Communism," read Bogart's official statement. "The reason I am flying to Washington is because I am an outraged and angry citizen who feels that my civil liberties are being taken away from me." The trip did little to help anyone's case—as Lauren later admitted in her memoir, "we certainly were naïve." The hostile reaction to their actions did little to diminish her convictions. Following the journey to Washington, Bacall published an editorial explaining her motives. "Why I Came to Washington" appeared in the *Washington Daily News* and was subsequently reprinted by newspapers around the country. "When they start telling you what pictures you can make, what your subjects can be, then it's time to rear up and fight!" the statement read in part. Bacall seemed less concerned than Bogie with the consequences her words and actions might have on her career. In the end, Bogie would back down, publishing another piece titled "I'm No Communist," distancing himself from the Hollywood Ten and denouncing his involvement with the Committee for the First Amendment. While Bacall stood by her husband, her politics would remain more radically liberal than his. In subsequent years, she'd be the one to introduce Bogie to the policies of Adlai Stevenson, which would lead to them becoming Stevenson's ardent supporters and campaigners. Lauren's involvement in his 1952 presidential bid would be much more personal than Bogie's. She traveled around the country to drum up support for Stevenson, often leaving her husband at home. "I was so in awe of him, and so enamored of him," she would say of Stevenson many decades later. "I'd never heard anyone in public life say what they really thought and say it the way Adlai Stevenson said it." Her fascination with Stevenson went beyond politics—he represented the passionate convictions and social conscience she herself now had. Despite her infatuation, there was to be no romance. Stevenson lost the 1953 election to Eisenhower, and he'd lose once again four years later. His lasting impact on Lauren would endure, both as a political influence and as her personal hero.

Bacall's political activities during the late 1940s and early 1950s certainly had the potential to harm her acting career. Those blacklisted during the period of the communist witch-hunt lost years and sometimes entire decades of work. And yet, she emerged from it mostly unscathed. She would remain a lifelong supporter of the Democratic Party and of liberal causes. In 1968, in the aftermath of the assassination of Robert Kennedy, she appeared on Dick Cavett's talk show to debate gun control. As the only woman on the panel, she bravely and decisively argued for the introduction of tougher gun laws, a debate which more than half-a-century later is still raging. "I'm a liberal and proud of it," she told Charlie Rose in 1994. "What's wrong with being a liberal? I think it's the best thing one can be. I'm a liberal and I'll stay one."

Even if her involvement with the Committee for the First Amendment didn't directly affect her standing in Hollywood, by the end of the 1940s her career was in trouble. She knew the only way to prove she could be more than "Bogie's Baby" was to get out of her Warners contract and find work elsewhere. This, however, wouldn't be so easy. The terms of her employment were far less flexible, not to mention lucrative, than Bogie's. She had little say in the kinds of projects she was given; whenever she rejected a script, she was put on suspension, only prolonging her commitment to the studio.

In 1949, mere months after the birth of Stephen, Warner cast Lauren as the second female lead in Michael Curtiz's *Young Man with a Horn*. Despite receiving second billing, after Kirk Douglas, it was in fact Doris Day who was the film's leading lady and Douglas's love interest. The part of Amy North wasn't sympathetic, and yet it was the more interesting one. The character is trapped within the constraints of her times—as a lesbian, an artist, and a restless spirit, she doesn't fit the mold of what society expects women to be. The film isn't kind or sensitive to her—as a queer character, she is portrayed as a deviant, a "sick girl," in tune with the consensus of the era. Interestingly, although her sexuality is fairly obvious to a modern viewer, at the time of the shoot, Lauren wasn't conscious of the fact she was playing a gay character. Curtiz, famous for directing Bogie in *Casablanca*, offered her little support in creating a multidimensional character. She was meant to be a villain of the story, a toxic character standing in the way of the movie's hero's self-realization, and his true love, Doris Day. Had she been directed by John Huston, she might have found a way to portray Amy with more nuance. Without guidance from her director or a full understanding of her character's motivation, the performance falls short of what it could have been. She's still effective; while her screen time is limited, each time she appears, the viewer is left wanting more. Once again, there's a hint, a promise of something under the surface, something that isn't fully realized by the film she's in.

Young Man with a Horn reunited Lauren with her old crush, Kirk Douglas. They were both big stars now, Douglas partly thanks to Lauren, who had mentioned his talent to the film's producer, Hal Wallis, back in 1946. Wallis had gone to New York to see Douglas in a play, liked what he saw, and signed him. Some of the old sparks might have been flying, but their friendship remained platonic. Watching Douglas and Bacall onscreen together is a joy, even if purely for aesthetic reasons. Sadly, they'd never have the chance to work together again.

Critics disliked *Young Man with a Horn*, and Lauren's performance. "The really ungrateful role in the picture is that which falls to the lot of Miss Bacall," read one review. "She seems quite unhappy with the part, and no one can honestly blame her." Audiences also stayed away, reinforcing the consensus that without Bogie by her side, Bacall was not a reliable draw. The last film she made on her Warners contract did little to alter this notion. *Bright Leaf*, again directed by Curtiz, and costarring Gary Cooper and Patricia Neal, was a dreary Western about a love triangle amidst North Carolina's tobacco fields. Once again, Curtiz fails to get the best out of his actors, and although the pairing of Bacall and Cooper should have been a major cinematic event, the result was a disappointment.

"Everyone thought I was terrific personally, but they stopped thinking of me as an actress," she would write about this period. "I was Bogie's wife, gave great dinners, parties, but work was passed over. It was frustrating. I wanted my career to go on."

With no work prospects on the horizon, Lauren decided to go on an adventure. Bogie was making another movie with John Huston, with Katharine Hepburn as his costar. They'd be shooting in London and on location in the Belgian Congo. Accompanying Bogie meant leaving their one-year-old son under the care of nurses and Natalie. She decided to go—a decision which would cause her some regrets in later years. And yet, the trip was to be one of the most unforgettable of her life, and the start of a lifelong friendship with Hepburn.

The African Queen would be one of the most successful films of its time—a huge box-office hit and a critical success, winning Bogart the Academy Award for best actor. Bogie's career had reached another peak. Meanwhile, Bacall's was all but dead.

CHAPTER 4

Unconventional Movie Star

LAUREN BACALL'S STAR PERSONA OF THE 1950S IS A COMPLICATED ONE. THE actress who had risen to stardom in the hard-boiled, shady world of noir suddenly found herself in a very different cinematic landscape. Independent women who challenged the male order were now seen as dangerous and undesirable—the boom of the 1950s was based on the idea of the nuclear family, with a strong patriarchal structure. The woman's role wasn't to present a threat to a man, but to support him. Throughout the decade, Bacall found herself struggling to fit in, fighting for roles and scripts which would suit her talents as well as her convictions.

That is not to say that she didn't manage to create some memorable performances—she tried a variety of genres and styles, leaving her mark on some of the most emblematic cinematic trends of the decade. And yet, there's an undeniable sense of an unrealized potential—portrayals of complicated and interesting women she could have brought to life, had she been given the chance to. Instead, the woman who had just a few short years earlier set the imagination of moviegoers ablaze with her mysterious, independent, and sexually charged persona would spend what was arguably her prime mostly playing docile wives—a sad reality that serves as a perfect illustration of the era's rigid and unequal gender politics.

It was also partly due to the fact that the public's perception of Lauren Bacall had shifted—she was now the perfect wife and mother, with a beautiful home and an all-American, Norman Rockwellesque domestic life. The public saw her as an ideal embodiment of postwar womanhood: beautiful, stylish, devoted to her husband. The industry too failed to recognize Bacall as more than simply Mrs. Humphrey Bogart. As a result, after the failure of *Bright Leaf,* Lauren stayed away from the screen for nearly three years, getting herself untangled from the Warners contract and attempting to find independent projects that would allow her to finally show what she was capable of. In 1952, shortly after the birth of Leslie, she was offered a contract with Twentieth Century-Fox, whose boss, the notorious Darryl F. Zanuck, assured her that the one-picture-a-year deal would guarantee quality material, tailor-made for her set of skills. It's unlikely Lauren believed him, especially since her agent had advised her against signing the contract, but with few other opportunities available, she decided to give it a chance.

The first project under the new contract would prove to be one of the most successful movies of her career—at least in terms of box-office receipts and the film's continued appeal. *How to Marry a Millionaire* was written by Nunnally Johnson—a talented writer and a friend of the Bogarts—and was inspired in part by Doris Lilly's 1951 book, *How to Meet a Millionaire,* as well as by two stage plays, Zoe Akins's *The Greeks Had a Word for It* and Katherine Albert's *Loco.* Lauren later claimed that she had personally suggested the idea to Zanuck after George Cukor had given her the Akins play to read. Fox intended the movie to be a big moneymaker, hoping to draw audiences away from television screens and into the movie theaters, which by 1953 was becoming increasingly difficult. In 1950, there were as many as eight million TV sets in the United States, and by 1957 the number would rise to forty-one million. Studios had to think of ways to attract audiences, luring them with promises of wonders that television couldn't provide. Visual spectacle was one such thing—big-budget epics were in vogue, and new technical inventions, such as Fox's CinemaScope, were designed to make the viewing experience all the more impressive. While the studio's 1953 biblical epic, *The*

Robe was currently being reshot in CinemaScope, *Millionaire* would be the first film to be shot entirely using the new technique.

But technical gimmicks such as the use of CinemaScope only got the studios so far—a far more reliable ingredient of success, and a far cheaper to produce, was good old-fashioned sex. Popular television shows in the 1950s were wholesome and family focused, and for a taste of the forbidden, a trip to the movies was still necessary, although the studios' publicity materials often promised more than was possible to deliver under the strict rules of the Production Code. To ensure *Millionaire*'s box-office potential, Fox decided to use two of its greatest sex symbols, Betty Grable and Marilyn Monroe. Grable had been the studio's top star for a number of years, and she had been one of the most popular pinups of the war years, rivalled only by Columbia's Rita Hayworth. By 1953, her popularity was dwindling, but she still possessed enough star power to boost a picture. Marilyn was continuing her meteoric rise to superstardom; her latest film, *Niagara*, premiered in January of 1953, causing a sensation. While Zanuck had a personal dislike of Monroe, he could not deny the public's insatiable appetite for her. Casting Marilyn opposite Grable almost guaranteed a smash.

How to Marry a Millionaire is a story of three New York models who decide to rent a posh Park Avenue apartment in hopes of meeting, and crucially marrying, rich men. The narrative is typical of the era: the ultimate goal for the female characters is marriage. There's never any question if marriage itself is the right choice—that's a given. The discourse focuses instead on *who* to marry—a rich man, or a poor one, marriage for love, or for security. With Monroe and Grable cast, Zanuck still had to find the third star to complete the movie's cast. In some ways, the character of Schatze Page is the most important to the movie's plot—she's the mastermind behind the whole scheme, and the one to whom the other two women look up. "I think she's the most intelligent person I guess I ever met," Grable's Loco declares in reference to Schatze in one of the film's early scenes.

Lauren was determined to be in the movie, believing it would put her career back on track. She expressed her interest to both Zanuck and the film's director, Jean Negulesco. With Zanuck's recent assurance that she'd be getting top quality material still fresh in her mind—not to mention the fact she had been the one to bring the story to Fox in the first place—Lauren was taken aback when Nunnally Johnson asked her to do a screen test for the role. She was further aggravated after finding out that neither of her costars had been required to test. Johnson tried to soften the blow by telling her that both Marilyn and Betty had previously proved themselves adept at playing comedy, while for Lauren the part marked a complete departure from her previous work—still, the idea of doing a screen test at this stage of her career was humiliating. She initially refused, but her desire to be in the film eventually outweighed her pride. She knew that chances like that didn't come along often, especially to her. Bogie too agreed that she ought to test. If Zanuck, Johnson, and Negulesco had harbored doubts about whether Lauren was right for the role, the test did more than convince them that Bacall *was* Schatze. The unique combination of her glamour and sophistication and the very authentic street smarts and impeccable comic timing was a revelation. She did her best to hide her nerves and "just how desperately" she wanted the part. After a weekend of biting her nails and waiting for the phone to ring, she was told she had the part.

Filming started in late February of 1953, while Bogie was in Italy shooting *Beat the Devil* with John Huston. It would be the first time that Lauren disregarded their agreement and put her own career above accompanying her husband on location. "I was selfish, pressing on with what I wanted to do," she would write in her memoir. "I enjoyed being able to do as I pleased for a while." Beyond the pleasure of sampling life without her husband, her decision was no doubt dictated by the fact that she wasn't quite ready to abandon her career, and she knew that if she wanted to be taken seriously as an actress and not seen as just Mrs. Bogart, she needed to work. At the time, a woman's desire to work was often judged to come at the expense of her family, and especially before the birth of the feminist movement, many suffered from crippling feelings of guilt. Bacall would come to wrestle with her own guilt in the years to come—for now, she was happy just to be resuming her career. Acting was still something she loved and wanted to dedicate herself to.

While she appreciated the quality of the material and the film's box-office potential, Lauren also recognized how sexist the premise of the story was. "Times have changed," she told a journalist. "Women are quite capable of making their own millions these days." Whatever her feelings about Johnson's script, she was determined to give the performance her all, which she did. From the very first scene, Bacall dominates the movie with her wit and dry humor, bringing her own personality and personal history to each scene. Schatze wasn't in fact that far removed from Betty Bacall, or at least, the way she might have been had her big break in movies not changed her life. Both were New York models; both hid their romantic natures behind a veneer of toughness. Schatze is also given some of the film's best lines, including her iconic response to "Do you seriously believe that having money automatically brings you happiness?" with "Well, no, but it doesn't automatically depress me either." Bacall also gets a chance to poke fun at her own taste for older men, when Schatze declares: "What I'm trying to tell you is that I've always liked older men. Look at Roosevelt. Look at Churchill. Look at that old fella, what's-his-name, in *African Queen*—absolutely crazy about him!"

And while in real life Bacall might have been content with Bogart, in the movie, Schatze eventually rejects William Powell (who was seven years Bogart's senior) in favor of a younger man, whom she believes to be a gas station attendant—in the end, of course, he turns out to be a millionaire.

Filming, for the most part, progressed smoothly. Lauren and Jean Negulesco became close, and he would go on to direct her in two more films while remaining a trusted friend for the rest of his life. Those who had expected the three stars to clash were in for a disappointment. All three women came into the movie with some degree of anxiety—Grable sensed that her time as a star was coming to an end, Monroe was quickly getting tired of the dumb blonde persona she was asked to recreate; yet again, and Bacall relied on *Millionaire* to get her career back on track. While all this tension could have easily proved explosive, instead, it brought the actresses closer. Lauren and Betty Grable both felt protective towards Marilyn, whose insecurities would often prevent her from leaving her dressing room, keeping the entire company waiting. "Grable and I decided we'd try to make it easier for her, make her feel she could trust us," Lauren later wrote. Since the movie was being filmed in CinemaScope, many of the scenes were longer, with the actors required to deliver more lines than had been customary in films. This terrified Marilyn, who looked to her coach, Natasha Lytess for approval, often asking for as many as fifteen takes before she was satisfied with her own performance. Not knowing which take would end up being used, Lauren had to give her all each time—as she described it in her memoir: "not easy—often irritating." "And yet I couldn't dislike Marilyn," she continued. "She had no meanness in her—no bitchery." For better or worse, Lauren would be asked about Marilyn for the rest of her life—perhaps second only to her relationship with Bogie, her experience of working with Monroe would be something interviewers remained most curious about. To her credit, no matter how tricky the questions, often designed to fish for a biting comment, Bacall was never anything less than generous. "She was sweet," she told Robert Osborne in 2005. "And the moment that camera turned on, she became this incredible creature—no question about that. She was just herself and she was absolutely dazzling as herself."

How to Marry a Millionaire premiered in November of 1953, with a glitzy opening at Fox's Wilshire Theatre in Beverly Hills. Lauren arrived with Bogie and Marilyn, the trio causing a sensation. Photos from the night, with Bogart sandwiched between the two glamour queens, appeared on front pages around the world, in subsequent years becoming iconic as the perfect illustration of the razzle-dazzle of Hollywood's Golden Age. The film itself divided critics. While some publications raved about it, with *Buffalo Courier Express* calling it an "impressive artistic achievement," Bosley Crowther of the *New York Times* was less generous, dismissing the film as "an average portion of very light comedy," and judging Bacall "cold and waspish"—hardly the praise she hoped for or deserved. Many critics faulted her for appearing less glamorous than her two costars, missing the sultriness of her noir days. "Miss Bacall was called The Look in her first film—however, her 'Look' (now) appears merely to be somewhat sullen," wrote one critic. Not yet thirty years old, and just two years older than Marilyn, Bacall was already facing the rampant ageism so prevalent at the time, especially in relation to female actors. In recent years, Bacall's performance has been reevaluated in a much more positive light—it's clear that she's the backbone of the movie.

Despite the mixed reviews, *Millionaire* became a huge box-office hit, just as Zanuck had hoped. Lauren, however, didn't benefit from the success as much as she had anticipated. The popularity of the film was credited mostly to the magic of Marilyn Monroe, whose fame seemed to be growing with each passing day. Her movie *Gentlemen Prefer Blondes,* which had come out in the summer, was already one of the biggest moneymakers of the year. Marilyn's romantic involvement with the Yankee legend Joe DiMaggio further elevated her status to that of America's most beloved star. Her name appeared ahead of Grable and Bacall on all promotional materials and her image took center stage on posters, luring audiences with a promise of more Marilyn. While Lauren didn't outwardly resent Marilyn, she couldn't help feeling jealous of her incredible popularity. "I don't like the moments of professional envy I have," she admitted years later. While *How to Marry a Millionaire* might not have proven as big a personal triumph as she had hoped, it remains one of Bacall's most popular movies. It allowed her, at least partly, to move away from the shadow of Bogie and her film noir days and step into the arena on her own.

• • •

As soon as she finished working on *Millionaire,* Lauren flew to Europe to be reunited with Bogie. She had hoped to join him in Italy but due to the delays in filming, she was to see him only in London. In her memoir, she recounts the joy of seeing her husband again following a three-month separation—"after eight years of marriage the excitement was as strong as ever." Despite her crush on Adlai Stevenson, for whom she'd been tirelessly campaigning the year prior, Lauren's love and loyalty for Bogie hadn't diminished. Reading her memoir, however, and examining the many interviews she would give in the decades following Bogie's death, it's evident that there existed a certain conflict in the marriage: as much as Bacall cherished her role of a loving wife, it seems that deep down she sensed that Bogie's rather old-fashioned and somewhat possessive attitude had prevented her from truly flourishing in her career. The conflict ran deeper than Bogie simply not wanting Lauren to go away on location or demanding that she accompany him on his—which was already a rather big sacrifice for her to make. At times it appears as though he was afraid that should Bacall have the opportunity to truly spread her creative wings, her success and fame might eclipse his. It's possible that, as Bacall on occasion suggested, he was simply afraid that should her career have taken center stage in her life, their marriage would not have survived. It was with *How to Marry a Millionaire* that Lauren's attitude toward her work shifted—from this point on, she would attempt to juggle her commitment to her husband and simultaneously do her best to fulfill her professional ambitions. Many years later, actress Jessica Lange, while reflecting on her own relationship with Sam Shepard, told Charlie Rose: "I recently had this conversation with Lauren Bacall. She told me her career suffered because Bogart never wanted her to work." Evidently, more than three decades after Bogie's death, Bacall continued to be haunted by the choices she had made. "After we were married for a few years, I really wasn't getting any decent offers, because everyone just thought of me as Bogie's wife," she reflected in 1985. "And then you say, wait a minute, I still want to act, I still want to do good things."

Back in the States, as she was preparing for the opening of *How to Marry a Millionaire*, Lauren was approached to leave her hand and footprints outside Grauman's Chinese Theater on Hollywood Boulevard—next to the Oscar, the filmdom's highest recognition. Bacall's refusal of the honor is curious. The statement released to the press at the time explained that she saw the honor as meant for those in the motion picture industry who were "unforgettables and irreplaceables"—neither of which she believed herself to be at this stage of her career. Back in 1946, she had been on her knees helping Bogie plant his footprints in the wet cement—now she was excluding herself from the ranks of film luminaries she longed to be accepted by. Perhaps unsurprisingly, the idea for Lauren to refuse actually came from Bogie. Bacall described it as him "loving the chance to puncture Hollywood's ego," however, it wasn't a chance he had been willing to take when it came to his own legend-building. It's hard to see the episode as anything other than Bogart's fear of puncturing *his* own ego—rather than expressing pride in his wife's success and championing her achievement the way she had done for him, he once again let his insecurity stand in the way of Lauren's professional triumph.

Some in the industry saw the act as evidence of Bacall's arrogance—others admired her gumption. Sidney Skolsky wrote in his column: "I have admiration for Bacall's honesty, not only in this but in other matters. It's time to start making the footprints in the forecourt of Grauman's Chinese Theatre more than a publicity stunt!"

"Time went by, and I wasn't asked again," Bacall would later write wistfully. "A tourist or aspiring actor going to Grauman's Chinese to see the legendary stars' footprints will not see mine—or miss them."

• • •

In January of 1954, Bogie traveled to Rome to begin work on *The Barefoot Contessa*. The script was written by Joseph L. Mankiewicz, the man behind *All About Eve*, and the highly coveted titular role was given to Ava Gardner. Lauren followed Bogart to Rome, once again playing the role of a dutiful wife accompanying her husband on location. The Bogarts stayed at the legendary Excelsior Hotel on Via Veneto, while Gardner chose to rent an apartment instead. Lauren hadn't known Ava before—like the rest of the world, she knew *of* her. Like Bacall, Gardner rose from the ranks of noir queens, managing to establish herself as one of the most popular actresses of the 1950s. Despite Bogie receiving top billing for *Contessa*, as well as a higher salary, the film was to be Gardner's triumph, thereafter symbolizing the pinnacle of her Hollywood career. Beside her acting credits, Gardner was making headlines for her turbulent marriage to Frank Sinatra, whom she had just left to pursue an independent life in Europe—as Lauren wrote in her memoir, "the first and only time someone else had done the leaving." Bacall arrived in Rome with a birthday cake she had carried all the way from New York—a gift to Ava from the still lovesick Sinatra. It was not a great way for the two women to meet, as Ava, furious with her estranged husband, gave Lauren the cold shoulder.

"She couldn't have cared less," Lauren wrote. "She wanted me to put it down on some table she indicated. No thank you, nothing. I was furious with her and never got to know her on that film."

She realized that Ava's behavior "had only to do with Frank"—in later years, the two stars would get a chance to get to know one another better and share a warm, if casual, acquaintanceship. At the time, however, there's no doubt Lauren harbored a note of professional envy towards Gardner. Both were former clients of Charlie Feldman, both had become major stars in film noir adaptations of Hemingway—Ava's breakthrough came in the 1946 hit *The Killers*. But while Lauren struggled to find her place in the cinematic universe of the 1950s, Ava reigned as one of the great sex goddesses of the decade, and one of the most sought-after stars. She was now headlining a star vehicle, playing the title role in a prestige production, directed by one of Hollywood's most esteemed auteurs, and acting opposite Lauren's husband. To a woman with Bacall's ambition and talent, it must have stung. It was by now becoming a pattern: she watched other actresses walk away with juicier parts, more hyped-up publicity, and the industry's accolades. Of course, it was universally acknowledged that she was striking and had an unbeatable style. She had the look, the voice, the personality. But above all, she was the wife of Humphrey Bogart. She would still need to prove to the public, the industry, and to herself, that she was more than just that.

• • •

Upon her return from Italy, Lauren started work on yet another Jean Negulesco-directed movie for Fox. *Woman's World* was an ensemble piece meant as a commentary on corporate America of the postwar years and the era's gender politics. Lauren's role was initially to be played by Gloria Grahame, Bogie's *In a Lonely Place* costar, but when Grahame dropped out, Zanuck turned to Bacall. It's hard to imagine what attracted Lauren to the project, other than the chance to work with an impressive group of actors. After the success of *How to Marry a Millionaire*, which relied heavily on Lauren's central performance, *Woman's World* was a step back. Bacall is billed fourth, after Clifton Webb, June Allyson, and Van Heflin, and her talent is wasted on a paper-thin character.

To any modern viewer, *Woman's World* will appear appallingly sexist. The movie tells the story of three male sales executives who travel to New York in order to compete for their company's top job. Their wives travel with them, aware they'll be scrutinized along with the men, although for very different reasons. The film follows the logic that behind every great man there's a docile and able woman, although, in the end, even that theory is disproved. Of the three female characters, only one (played by Arlene Dahl) displays any kind of ambition of her own—she is, however, also the least sympathetic, and to put it mildly, morally reprehensible. Lauren plays Elizabeth Burns, a former model who agrees to accompany her estranged husband (played by Fred MacMurray) only for the sake of appearances—in reality, their marriage is over due to her husband's workaholism. Bacall does her best to inject some life and a touch of humor into her character, but in the end, she's not able to save the film. Perhaps not surprisingly, she would completely omit mentioning *Woman's World* from both of her books, and she would rarely discuss the film in subsequent years.

Despite its weaknesses, at the time of its release *Woman's World* was well-received critically, and a moderate box-office success. In line with the times, critics didn't question the gender dynamics, seeing the film as light and glossy entertainment. After doing decent business, the movie would disappear into obscurity, rarely resurfacing on TV screens in the decades since.

Lauren's contract with Fox failed to resurrect her career in a way she had hoped. Although *Millionaire* had been a hit, she didn't see *Woman's World* as a worthy follow-up: it was not a star vehicle, and her part could have been played by any other contract star. Drifting on the open waters of freelancing once more, she agreed to appear in another ensemble piece. This one, titled rather unfortunately *The Cobweb*, would be her first time at the prestigious Metro Goldwyn Mayer, and she was to be directed by the esteemed Vincente Minnelli, the former husband of her good friend Judy Garland. It is likely that Bacall's decision to be in the film had more to do with her desire to keep herself visible rather than with the quality of the material: the script is a rather melodramatic and convoluted soap opera about the goings on at an upscale mental health clinic, with the plot, typical of Minnelli, at times stirring towards the absurd. Bacall does not get the showiest part; the film's female lead is played by Gloria Grahame. The few scenes in which Minnelli allows Lauren to shine, however, she truly does, and the camera loves her. Perhaps the film's most memorable moment occurs at the midway point, when Bacall's character, in response to Richard Widmark's "You're young, you've got a whole world ahead of you," delivers the eerily prophetic line, "It's up against real competition—with the one behind me." Within a couple of years, she'd be living these words in a way she never could have imagined.

When the film came out in the summer of 1955, it made little impact at the box office and the reviews were mixed. It seemed that Lauren was moving further away from the sort of work she'd been hoping for. She wasn't at the top of any producer's list when it came to casting important roles. Younger stars, like Elizabeth Taylor, were drawing crowds to the theaters, and projects would be built around them. Lauren saw her situation as frustrating and unfair—she was merely thirty-one, and, she felt, at the top of her game, yet there seemed to be no one left in Hollywood who would recognize that. She wrote letters to friends, dropping hints, asking to be considered for projects—a position which couldn't have been easy. "Never having done this before I'm not quite sure how to begin," she wrote to Joseph L Mankiewicz. "Of course, it's about *Guys and Dolls* and Miss Adelaide. I'd love to play the part and would very much appreciate if you would give me some thought." As it turns out, Lauren wasn't the only one reaching out to Mankiewicz with the request to play Adelaide—Marilyn Monroe had also telephoned him about it. In the end, the part went to Vivian Blaine, who had originated the character in the Broadway production and would be the only cast member from the show to make it into the film version.

Some of the best work of this period came to Lauren not from cinema, but surprisingly, from television. Having expressed their disinterest in the new medium only a few years prior, by 1955, the Bogarts, like many other major Hollywood players, had come to recognize the power of television in maintaining their popularity. The general attitude had shifted from disdain and mistrust to an if-you-can't-beat-them-join-them approach. Their first joined foray into the small screen would also prove to be their last onscreen pairing. The project was an adaptation of Robert E. Sherwood's 1935 play, *The Petrified Forest*. Starring in the original Broadway production had been a career breakthrough for Bogie, and his performance in the 1936 film adaptation, opposite Leslie Howard and Bette Davis, had set him on the course to movie stardom. Now, two decades later, he was to reprise his role as the gangster Duke Mantee, with Henry Fonda as the failed writer Alan Squier, originally played by Howard, and Lauren as the dreamy waitress Gabrielle, who in the film version had been played by her idol, Bette Davis. "It was a part no one in the movie world would have cast me in," she later wrote.

Both Bogie and Bacall had reservations about appearing in the production, which was set to be broadcast live on May 30, 1955. Bogie, however, had the advantage of knowing the role of Duke Mantee inside out, having played it onstage, in the movie version, and later on the radio. His extensive theater experience also helped; performing the entirety of a play before an audience came naturally to him. For Lauren, the whole experience was terrifying, and yet, she saw it as a challenge and as a chance to prove herself a capable actor rather than just a glamorous star. The role of Gaby marked a significant departure from the parts she'd been playing on the big screen, especially since leaving Warners.

Sherwood's sensitive writing gave her the opportunity to portray a set of complex emotions, to build a character from the inside. She was also playing against type: Gabrielle isn't worldly or sophisticated in the matters of sex. She's a dreamer, a small-town girl who recites poetry and longs to travel to France and become an artist—as Bacall rightly noted, not the sort of role she was likely to be offered in movies.

While Bogart receives top billing, it is the relationship between Fonda and Bacall which constitutes the heart of the story, and their scenes in the production are filled with tenderness and nuance. Despite her nerves, Lauren manages to create a convincing and often moving performance. At times, her lack of experience shows—particularly in the closing scene, with Fonda dying in her arms, Lauren seems unable to reach the emotional heights the moment demands. Had she been afforded the luxury of multiple takes, she might have fared better, although limitations in her dramatic range would at times resurface in her later movie work.

The Petrified Forest was shown as part of NBC's acclaimed *Producer's Showcase* anthology, and it became a ratings success. Reviews were mostly positive, although not all the critics loved Bacall. Some thought she was too old for the part; others compared her unfavorably to Davis. None thought to question the age of Fonda or Bogart—both were some two decades older than their characters in the play. For her part, Lauren refused to let the critics get to her. "I was a romantic dreamer, and I was good, dammit," she would later write. She loved acting opposite Fonda, and she saw the experience as an important step in her artistic development.

A year later, she would once again come back to television, this time at the request of Noel Coward, who wanted her to play Elvira in the production of his play *Blithe Spirit*. For Lauren, the offer was a sort of cosmic joke—she had been an usher during the 1942 run of the play at the Morosco Theater, where the part of Elvira was played by Leonora Corbett. Now she was to star opposite Coward himself, with a cast that also included Claudette Colbert and the brilliant Mildred Natwick. Once again, the experience was nerve-wracking for Lauren, although she enjoyed working with Coward and playing light comedy was a welcome change for her. During rehearsals, Coward would often clash with Colbert in what to Lauren seemed little more than a battle of two inflated egos. The plot required Colbert to resent the younger Bacall, which, it seemed, came to the actress rather naturally. For the live taping of the production, Coward invited an array of Hollywood luminaries, including Elizabeth Taylor and Judy Garland, which obviously only added to the anxious energy that surrounded the entire enterprise.

Lauren plays the ghost of Coward's first wife who is summoned during a spiritual seance and comes to haunt him along with his current spouse, Colbert. She appeared playful and relaxed, flirtatious and capricious—in short, the perfect Coward heroine. She also looked stunning in a goddess-like chiffon gown and a blond wig, lending the production the glamorous touch Coward was after. Her style and mannerisms at times evoke similarities with that of her friend Vivien Leigh—who would herself be appearing in Coward's *South Sea Bubble* on the West End stage in the same year.

Blithe Spirit was shown on January 14, 1956, and was another ratings success for Lauren. She was more confident than she had been the first time around and the light nature of the material seemed to suit her talents. Coward, with his usual bite, later wrote in his diary: "Bacall is charming and no trouble, also, unfortunately, no comedienne, but she moves beautifully, looks ravishing, and tries like mad."

CHAPTER 5

The Most Famous Widow in the World

BY THE MID-1950S, LAUREN'S CAREER SEEMED TO BE HEADING IN THE RIGHT direction, at long last. She experienced success on TV with two well-received productions, *The Petrified Forest* and *Blithe Spirit*, and her film career was also getting a significant boost with her appearance as John Wayne's leading lady in *Blood Alley* in 1955 and having a lead in Douglas Sirk's *Written on the Wind* the following year. For a while it seemed like things were looking up—both her work and her domestic life with Bogie, Stephen, and Leslie were sources of joy. Things were about to take a tragic turn though, throwing Bacall's well-ordered life upside down. For the time being, she had no clue or premonition of what was coming.

That's not to say that her marriage to Bogie had been nothing but smooth sailing all the way. There were times when both strayed, even if only emotionally, rather than physically. Bacall later admitted that due to her young age and inexperience at the time of her marriage, she was prone to being attracted to men who impressed her on an intellectual level—Adlai Stevenson and Leonard Bernstein being the two obvious examples. She also enjoyed the company of younger men whose attentions excited her and made her feel desirable. There's nothing to suggest that any of these relationships ever went beyond flirtatious friendships. The same can't be said for Bogie. While Bacall herself went to her grave maintaining her late husband's impeccable moral character, rumors of Bogart's long-term affair with his personal secretary/hairdresser/toupee-maker Verita Thompson circulated even during his lifetime. Thompson would eventually claim that she had been the legendary actor's mistress for most of the duration of his marriage to Bacall, detailing the relationship in her 1982 memoir, *Bogie and Me*, and calling herself "Bacall's worst nightmare." Little evidence exists to support her claims of a long-standing physical affair, but there can be no doubt that a close relationship between the two was real, dating back to the years of Bogart's stormy union with Mayo Methot. There are numerous articles and photos from the 1950s confirming Thompson's presence on the set of all of Bogart's films from the time, and she even appears to have been friendly with Lauren and close to the Bogart children. For her part, Lauren never publicly acknowledged or addressed the Verita Thompson story. It isn't certain to what extent she had been aware of the relationship during Bogie's lifetime or how she felt about it; whatever her feelings on the subject, she would keep them to herself for the rest of her life.

• • •

Blood Alley was to be coproduced by Warner Bros and John Wayne's newly established Batjac Productions. The film was based on Albert Sidney Fleischman's novel, with the author also penning the script. Drawing on his own experiences in the Navy during World War II, Fleischman's story was vivid and full of colorful characters, promising a first-rate motion picture. Lauren lobbied to be cast as the film's female lead, Cathy Grainger, hoping she and Bogie could make this their big screen comeback. While for a time Bogart was considered by the studio to play the movie's hero, his standard salary at the time was $500,000, significantly higher than the film's modest budget allowed for. The studio turned instead to Robert Mitchum, whose brooding screen presence would have no doubt paired well with Bacall's trademark sultriness.

She was excited at the prospect of acting opposite Mitchum, and the company assembled in the San Francisco Bay area, which stood in for the waterways of China, where the filming was set to begin in January of 1955. Within a matter of days, Mitchum was either fired or made to quit the film—accounts vary. The official story at the time suggested that Mitchum, a heavy drinker and pot smoker, got into a brawl with one of the crew members. John Wayne's daughter later remembered her father telling her that it was William Wellman, the film's director, who "drove Mitchum to quit." With no leading man, the studio desperately looked for a replacement, turning to Gregory Peck, who declined. Eventually, Wayne himself was forced to step in and take on the role of Captain Wilder—an American merchant marine who leads a group of two hundred Chinese villagers out the communist-occupied China and into freedom in the British port of Hong Kong. The film was seen as thinly veiled anticommunist propaganda, and Wayne's presence in the movie only made the message more pronounced. Bacall's desire to be part of the film is curious—it's possible that she saw it as a way to soften her image and prove, once and for all, that despite her liberal politics, she was not a communist sympathizer. Most likely though, she simply saw her part as a strong one—which, for all the film's many faults, it was.

Wayne disliked his role and felt himself miscast. The character of the cynical captain would have certainly suited Bogie better, as it would have Mitchum. Wellman's old-fashioned direction did little to utilize whatever chemistry existed between Lauren and Wayne. Their scenes carry the promise of something exciting bubbling under the surface, but the film never delivers on it. Midway through filming, the director was taken ill, forcing Wayne to take over and quite literally stir the ship through treacherous waters. In the end, Lauren's performance remains one of the only highlights of this otherwise disappointing production. She skillfully communicates both her character's strength and vulnerability, remaining natural despite the sometimes less than believable mise-en-scene. There are moments that allow her to do what Bacall does best—take control of a situation, defy the male ego, and

Lauren Bacall, "the Look," 1944. (From the collection of Michael Gregg Michaud.)

Bacall's early publicity photos highlighted her image as a confident and sophisticated woman—an image she struggled to live up to. (From the collection of Benjamin Meißner.)

Lauren Bacall embodied the ideal of wartime womanhood in America. (From the collection of Michael Gregg Michaud.)

Love is in the air: Bogart and Bacall on the set of *The Big Sleep*, their second onscreen pairing. The film is today considered one of the finest examples of film noir, 1945. (From the collection of Michael Gregg Michaud.)

Lauren Bacall became one of the emblematic female stars of the postwar years. Here, her beauty is captured by studio publicity photographers. (From the collection of Michael Gregg Michaud.)

Bogie and Bacall on their wedding day, May 21, 1945. (From the collection of Michael Gregg Michaud.)

Happy days: Bogie and Bacall in love. (From the collection of Michael Gregg Michaud.)

Upon marrying Bogart, Bacall became part of Hollywood's royalty. Yet Warner Bros. had little idea of how to utilize her talent. (From the collection of Michael Gregg Michaud.)

Bogie and Bacall in Washington, DC, in October 1947, leading the Committee for the First Amendment. They had come to the nation's capital to show support for those targeted by the House Un-American Activities Committee. (Photofest.)

Following several lackluster projects and studio suspensions, Lauren knew that the only way to save her career was to leave Warner Bros. (From the collection of Michael Gregg Michaud.)

Lauren with her son, Stephen Humphrey Bogart. (From the collection of Michael Gregg Michaud.)

Key Largo, released in 1948, was to be the last onscreen pairing of Bogart and Bacall. Lauren's performance is restrained yet powerful, with moments of inspired melancholy brilliantly captured by director John Huston. (Photofest.)

The Bogarts in the early 1950s. Bogie's career had just reached new heights, Bacall's was stalling. (From the collection of Michael Gregg Michaud.)

One of Bacall's best-loved films remains *How to Marry a Millionaire* from 1953. Her big comeback performance opposite Marilyn Monroe and Betty Grable proved that she could also play comedy. (From the collection of Michael Gregg Michaud.)

Belgian poster for *How to Marry a Millionaire*. Marilyn Monroe notably takes center stage as her popularity during this period soared. (From the collection of Benjamin Meißner.)

The premiere of *How to Marry a Millionaire*, Lauren with Bogie and Marilyn Monroe. The three represented all the glamour of Hollywood's Golden Age. (From the collection of Michael Gregg Michaud.)

Bogie and Bacall: the most iconic of all Classic Hollywood couples. (From the collection of Michael Gregg Michaud.)

The 1950s was a challenging decade for Bacall, both professionally and privately. (From the collection of Benjamin Meißner.)

Lauren Bacall, the epitome of a glamorous movie star of the 1950s. (From the collection of Benjamin Meißner.)

The gloriously over-the-top *Written on the Wind* is today regarded as one Douglas Sirk's masterpieces. At the time of its release, critics were polarized, and Bacall herself never much liked the film. Pictured her with her costar, Rock Hudson, 1956. (Photofest.)

Lauren at a Hollywood party, sitting between Bogie and Frank Sinatra. (From the collection of Michael Gregg Michaud.)

Lauren's brilliant comedic performance in *Designing Woman*, opposite her friend Gregory Peck, is all the more commendable considering the painful time she was going through at home, 1957. (Photofest)

A publicity portrait taken to promote *The Gift of Love*, the first movie Lauren shot after Bogie's death, 1958. (From the collection of Michael Gregg Michaud.)

Following Bogie's death, Lauren's friendship with Sinatra turned into an ill-fated romance. (From the collection of Michael Gregg Michaud.)

A backstage visit from a dear friend, Vivien Leigh, during the Broadway run of *Cactus Flower*. (From the collection of Greta Ritchie.)

Bacall was a scene stealer in Sydney Lumet's all-star adaptation of Agatha Christie's *Murder on the Orient Express*. Pictured here with her costar, Ingrid Bergman, 1974. (Photofest)

Lauren Bacall continued to work throughout the 1990s and beyond. Retirement never seemed like an option. (From the collection of Benjamin Meißner.)

Bacall earned her sole Oscar nomination for her memorable performance as Barbra Streisand's mother in *The Mirror Has Two Faces*, 1996. (From the collection of Michael Gregg Michaud.)

Even when her film roles became fewer and smaller in scale, her star power never dwindled. As much as she disliked being called a legend, she had unequivocally earned the title. (Photofest.)

assert her own agency. "Don't ever try ordering me around, Captain Wilder. And keep your hands to yourself!" she warns Wayne in one of the early scenes. At her cinematic best, not even the Duke could mess with Lauren Bacall.

Blood Alley was not well received by critics, and it failed to attract a large audience. Lauren was one of the only elements of the movie to be praised, with the *New York Times* describing her as "cool and statuesque" and calling her performance a "workmanlike stint." There are moments in the film that suggest what she might have been capable of—once again, though, the shallow script lets her down. Beyond showcasing her beauty and obvious star charisma, there's little opportunity for her to shine.

Written on the Wind, which went into production soon after the release of *Blood Alley*, would prove a more successful venture. The film was to be directed by Douglas Sirk, the German director who had recently had a hit with *All That Heaven Allows*, which, along with *Giant*, had turned Rock Hudson into a star. Sirk's reputation as one of the leading auteurs of the era wouldn't be established for another two decades; at the time he was simply seen as a reliable director, able to deliver a crowd-pleasing melodrama. Lauren had doubts about accepting the part of Lucy Moore. While she would be the female lead, her character, as written, appeared bland and unflashy, especially when contrasted with Dorothy Malone's neurotic Marylee Hadley. She also saw the script as an over-the-top soap opera, not anticipating that Sirk's vision would transform it into a cinematic masterpiece. She was, however, excited at the prospect of acting opposite Rock Hudson, whom Sirk cast as the film's male lead, and she agreed to be in the film. Like Lauren, Hudson had doubts about his part—he would once again be portraying a handsome, honest "good guy," while the more complex and challenging role of the film's antihero would go instead to Robert Stack. Hudson saw it as a repeat of the *Giant* dynamic: he had been the lead there too, but the film was stolen from him by James Dean's brilliant supporting turn. Bacall knew all too well what it felt like to be overshadowed. She had seen Gloria Grahame chew up the scenery (along with the drapes) in *The Cobweb*, and Arlene Dahl steal scenes in *Woman's World*—now it was Dorothy Malone's turn to walk away with some of the film's campiest moments, and with an Oscar for best supporting actress. And yet Lauren's more restrained performance constitutes the emotional backbone of the movie. There are subtle and genuine moments of pathos in her acting; she is moving and believable, refusing to get carried away by the artificiality of Sirk's cinematic world.

For years, critics have been less than generous in their assessment of Bacall's performance in *Written on the Wind*. Even as the film itself underwent a major critical reevaluation, the general consensus remained that Bacall "sleepwalked through the film," as Laura Mulvey put it. In fact, the balance of the picture rests on her shoulders. When viewed carefully, it's easy to see how much Sirk depends on Bacall's skill to achieve the emotional poignancy necessary for Malone and Stack to shine in their roles. Lauren showcases maturity and a nuanced understanding of her character's emotional life, no doubt aided by the growing anxieties in her own life, as it was around the time of the making of the film that Bogie's health began to deteriorate.

Written on the Wind was shot on Universal's lot in Hollywood through the winter months of 1955 and early 1956. There, Sirk carefully created his signature universe, full of color and fury. Lauren worked hard on the film, while also simultaneously preparing for the live taping of *Blithe Spirit*, which was scheduled to take place in January. She certainly had a lot on her plate, but she seemed to be thriving. Work had always been important to her, and she often used it as a distraction from facing any uncomfortable feelings and problems in her everyday life.

• • •

Bogie was coughing a lot. His cough had been an issue for a long time—back in 1954, during the making of *The Barefoot Contessa* in Rome, after numerous takes had to be repeated, Ava Gardner had asked him to see a doctor. He didn't. Now another friend, Greer Garson, expressed her concern. "You better see Dr. Maynard Brandsma, my internist at the Beverly Hills Clinic," she told him. Seeing him hesitate, Garson personally "dragged" Bogart to see the physician, as Lauren later wrote. "I should have realized at once that the mere fact that he'd consented to go with Greer to a doctor was indicative of something serious," Lauren reflected in her memoir. She was used to his coughing, and didn't think it could be anything more than a "smoker's cough"—everyone smoked in those days, and hardly anyone talked of, or knew about, the health risks involved. Tests were quickly performed, and the news wasn't good—there were cancerous cells in Bogie's esophagus, and an operation to remove them was urgently needed. In her memoir, Lauren wrote about the anguish of the days and weeks that followed: the long surgery, the fear of losing Bogie, the lengthy recovery period, first at the hospital and then at home. The children were too young to really understand what was happening, although, in hindsight, Lauren reflected that she, too, hadn't been aware of just how serious the situation was. During those weeks of uncertainty, which slowly turned into months, she was by Bogie's side constantly, holding his hand, tending to his every need. Friends were there to lend support too—Frank Sinatra and John Huston, Spencer Tracy and Katharine Hepburn, and others. It became clear that Bogart had been a much-loved figure in the industry, even for those who had perhaps only worked with him once or knew him briefly. They, too, were now reaching out with words of concern and support. While the surgery to remove the cancerous cells appeared successful, Bogie wasn't getting better. After a course of chemotherapy, he appeared weaker and thinner than ever. Plans for a movie version of John P. Marquand's novel, *Melville Goodwin*, which Warners planned to produce as a vehicle for Bogie and Bacall, had to be shelved. Sadly, they would never again appear on screen together. Bogie was disappointed; he wanted to go back to work, looking forward to coproducing *The Good Shepard* through his Santana production company. All these plans had to be put on hold indefinitely. As Lauren later remembered, there was never any mention of anything other than this being a passing illness; there was never any doubt about Bogie eventually getting better.

As spring turned into summer, something of a routine developed in the house on Mapleton Drive. As is often the case with long-term illness, its very presence becomes a mundane part of the everyday. The human capacity to normalize and accept things is astonishing. Looking after Bogie and trying to make sure that the effect of his illness on the children was minimal was a full-time job, despite a procession of doctors and nurses who were always coming in and out of the house. Every evening, a couple of friends would drop by for a drink and to check in on Bogie—and on her too. Sinatra was an almost daily visitor. His friendship was a source of strength to Lauren, and it was clear that he cared deeply about the Bogarts. As her birthday was approaching in September, Sinatra planned a party for her at The Sands in Las Vegas, where he would be performing. The star-studded guest list included Cole Porter, Kim Novak, David Niven, the Romanoffs, and other close friends. Bogie decided to give the bash a miss—he wasn't strong enough to attend a crowded event, choosing instead to spend a weekend onboard the Santana with Stephen. Lauren felt guilty about leaving Bogie, but later called the weekend her way of "escaping from reality." She certainly needed and deserved the break. Whether or not her feelings for Sinatra at this point were anything other than friendship isn't clear, although some have claimed that her dependency on him was bordering on obsessive infatuation. He represented the strength and confidence she craved at the time, and with the kind of attention he paid her, it's easy to see how her feelings could deepen. At The Sands, he sang "Happy Birthday" to her from the stage, before presenting her with a huge cake that read "Happy Birthday Den Mother," a humorous nod to her Rat Pack nickname. The press loved writing about the Rat Pack, which at the time included Judy Garland and Syd Luft, the Nivens, and others, and represented "probably the world's most exclusive group." Bacall was credited with coming up with the name—she was watching the news one evening and heard an LAPD officer referring to a group of teenage delinquents as a rat pack and glancing over at the characters assembled in her own living room, she laughed: "I think we should call this group of adult delinquents the Holmby Hills Rat

Pack." The Bogarts were at the heart of this exclusive set, although, after Bogie's death, Sinatra would take over, and the original cast of characters as well as the group's ethos would almost entirely change.

During the months of Bogie's illness, Lauren's career was at a standstill. The few offers she received had to be turned down—she simply couldn't imagine leaving Bogie and the kids. By the summer, however, his condition seemed stable enough—although without much improvement—for her to start to think about working again. She was approached with a project that had originally been developed for Grace Kelly—it was a comedy, with a plot resembling the 1942 Hepburn-Tracy classic, *Woman of the Year*. With her engagement to Prince Rainier of Monaco, Kelly was forced to drop out, at which point James Stewart, who was set to star opposite her, also withdrew. Produced by MGM, the idea for *Designing Woman* was said to have come from Helen Rose, the studio's head costume designer—thus, unsurprisingly, the premise involves a love story between a renowned female fashion designer and a sportswriter. Scriptwriter George Wells had observed Rose and her husband, Harry, at many industry parties and was inspired by what he saw: Rose thrived among the creative types, her husband often standing aside without much to talk about.

Lauren wasn't the only actress considered for the part, but she fought hard to get it, seeing it as an opportunity to flex her acting muscles and prove her abilities as a skilled comedienne. She agreed to a reduced salary, and she personally lobbied with the producer, Dore Schary, who was quickly won over by her enthusiasm. Bogie too encouraged her to do it, and she was delighted when Gregory Peck signed on as the male lead. Many years before, she had been an usherette at the Lyceum Theatre where the young Peck was getting his start. He had noticed her then and never forgot her. Later in Hollywood, they had met on occasion socially and there had always been a spark of chemistry between them—she was certain that they'd make a great onscreen couple. Vincente Minnelli, who had directed her in *The Cobweb*, was assigned to the film and Lauren was happy to work with him again. Her part in *The Cobweb* hadn't been substantial enough for them to truly have a chance to get to know each other, although Minnelli did his best to showcase Bacall's beauty and charisma in those few good scenes she had been given. Paradoxically, although filmed during one of the most difficult periods in Lauren's life, *Designing Woman* would prove one of the most rewarding and enjoyable projects of her career.

There was much anticipation for the movie, which was seen by the press as a prestigious production, with Helen Rose naturally set to design the wardrobe. As a personal friend of Lauren's, Rose came up with some truly breathtaking outfits for her, creating a series of unforgettable looks that would forever cement Bacall's status as a style icon. In September, the Associated Press announced excitedly that "the screen's first complete fashion show of ballroom gowns is being designed by Academy Award winner, Helen Rose, for Lauren Bacall in *Designing Woman*."

After a few weeks of costume fittings and camera tests, filming officially began in mid-September. The first day the company shot at the Beverly Hills Hotel, just down the road from the Bogarts, and Bogie was able to come to the set to watch his wife at work. He brought the children too and it was a rare happy moment for the whole family. Later, as filming moved to Marina Del Rey, where Lauren and Peck's characters start falling in love on board a rented boat, Bogie sailed over on the *Santana*, where the three stars enjoyed a carefree lunch break. The scenes shot on the boat must have been particularly bittersweet for Lauren, as they so resembled the home movies of her and Bogie onboard the *Santana*. She was still in denial, not allowing herself to think that her life with him was ending. Driving to the studio each day, and playing comedy with Peck, saved her. The script was filled with hilarious situations and plenty of physical comedy—running, screaming, fighting—and the two had a blast, forming a tight bond in the process, a friendship which was to last up until Peck's death in 2003.

"Aside from her professionalism in that film, I witnessed first-hand a side of Betty that meets the challenges of this world with elegance, humor, and above all, a kind of gallantry under fire," Peck said many years later in a TCM tribute to Bacall. "Bogie was desperately ill by this point, but Betty came to the set each day, somehow masking her feelings, and delivering the goods when the camera rolled."

Given the circumstances, Lauren's sparkling comic turn in the film is a true revelation. That she was able to so completely lose herself in the often-outrageous silliness of the fictional scenario is a testament both to her skill as an actress and the resilience of the human spirit. Bacall's performance is close to being note-perfect—her timing is impeccable, and she's able to be warm and loving, insanely jealous, angry: whatever the moment demands. She's authentic, even when dressed in Rose's over-the-top costumes, including the now-iconic all-mink dress she wears in the scene at a boxing match. The film is without a doubt a celebration of Helen Rose, and yet at no point do the clothes take over from Bacall's performance—*she* wears the clothes, they do not wear her.

As filming continued into October and November of 1956, things at home looked increasingly bleak. In early December, Bogie's medical team, led by Dr. Brandsma, finally sat Lauren down. Bogie's cancer had spread throughout his body, they told her. All treatments had failed. It was time to face the truth: Bogie wouldn't last much longer; in fact, they were surprised he had lasted this long. They spent the Christmas of 1956 at home; Lauren doing her best to keep the children happy. Bogie turned fifty-seven—his final birthday, his last Christmas. And still, the inevitable was never mentioned. Lauren wasn't sure how much Bogie knew, but she admired him more than ever—his strength and complete lack of self-pity, no matter how much pain and physical discomfort he was facing. Friends continued to visit, although Lauren had to impose limits to make sure Bogie got his rest. Kate and Spence were the only ones allowed to stay longer, as they had always had a soothing effect on both Bogie and Lauren. People like Jack Warner, Sam Goldwyn, and David Selznick also came to pay a visit to one of Hollywood's greats. On Saturday, January 12, Hepburn and Tracy came to see Bogie as usual. As they were leaving, Hepburn kissed him goodnight, as she always had, but this time felt different. Bogie looked up at Tracy, who had put his hand on the frail actor's shoulder, and said, "Goodbye, Spence." "You could tell he meant it," Hepburn later remembered. "He'd always said 'goodnight' before. When we were downstairs, Spence looked at me, and said, 'Bogie's going to die.'" That night, Bogie asked Lauren to stay by his side; during the months of his illness, she had stayed in the small room adjacent to the bedroom. Now, she lay by him and held his hand, but she slept very little that night, as Bogie restlessly tossed and kept picking at his chest. The next morning, he said it had been the worst night of his life. As Lauren prepared to drive the children to Sunday school, Bogie looked at her: "Goodbye, Kid. Hurry back." By the time she returned not long after, Bogie had fallen into a coma, from which he wouldn't wake up. He died in the early hours of January 14. Humphrey Bogart, the man, was gone. Bogie, the legend, was born. The nurse went into the small room, just off the actor's bedroom, to gently awaken Lauren. "Mrs. Bogart, it's all over. Mr. Bogart has died."

• • •

Humphrey Bogart's death was big news all over the world. He had been one of the emblematic stars of Hollywood's dream factory, his face instantly recognizable, the persona he created celebrated and emulated by a new generation of actors. The papers noted that the assemblage of celebrated names at his memorial service was "one of the largest funeral crowds in years." But there were no stars inside the All-Saints Episcopal Church in Beverly Hills that day: they were simply colleagues, friends, people who had known and loved the man. John Huston delivered the eulogy, which was simple, poignant, filled with love and admiration, not just for Bogart's talent as an actor, but also for the bravery he had shown in the face of death. Among those who had gathered to pay their respects were Hepburn and Tracy, Gregory Peck, Marlene Dietrich, Errol Flynn, Gary Cooper, James Mason, and Charles Boyer. Sinatra was notably absent—a singing engagement had kept him in New York. In the front row sat the actor's widow along with their two children. She was pale and beautiful, numb from the pain and shock of what had happened, going through the motions of the day's rituals. She would later reflect that the only lucid thought she had during that time was to place a model of the *Santana* at the altar—a poignant symbol of Bogie's love of freedom and the sea. As the service was taking place, Bogart's body was being cremated and a simple urn Lauren had selected would later be laid to rest at the Forest Lawn cemetery, the final resting place of so many who, like Bogie, had contributed to the creation of the Hollywood mythology. After the service, Lauren returned to the big house on Mapleton Drive, along with the dozens of friends who came to reminisce.

More than a thousand letters and telegrams came from all over the country, and from across the world. Radio and TV ran tributes to Bogart, as did all the newspapers, for days to come. After that, it all went quiet. As dust began to settle around her, Lauren realized that she was alone, for the first time in her life. She had to stay strong for the children, and for herself. Allowing herself to grieve properly was not an option she felt was available to her. Friends offered advice and words of wisdom—go back to work, the sooner the better. Moss Hart wrote her a letter cautioning against mourning; "In spite of the death, you're a lucky woman," Hart wrote. "It is a lucky woman indeed who can enrich a man's life to the extent that you enriched Bogie's, and now is the time to remember that." The magnitude of the loss of Bogie was something that would take her years to recognize and to heal from. Beyond the heartbreak of losing the man she loved deeply, she would also have to face the harsh realities of being not only a woman on her own but also an actor in an industry which had always seen her as Mrs. Humphrey Bogart. Could she make it just as Lauren Bacall? In a way, she was back to being the eighteen-year-old Betty Bacall again—shy, awkward, wanting to be noticed, to be appreciated, to be loved.

"Life every so often behaves as though it had seen too many bad movies," Bogart once said in *The Barefoot Contessa*. Over the next months, Lauren was to find out just how true the line was. For the time being, she stayed in California. Pretty soon though, she found facing the memories of Bogie, which were scattered all over the house on Mapleton Drive, unbearable. During the weeks after his death, *Written on the Wind* went into general release all over the country and it was playing to packed theaters. Reviews were mixed but crowds flocked to see it, making it a big box-office hit. Critics tended to single out Dorothy Malone and Robert Stack, but it was Lauren whose name, along with Hudson's, was above the title—she was the star of the picture, and she had a smash on her hands. It was an unexpected and welcome turn of events—she very much needed a boost, and if her personal life lay in tatters, at least she could feel pride in her professional achievement. More good news was to come later that spring as *Designing Woman* opened in May to a warm critical reception, becoming another success at the box office. The film may not be as well-remembered today as it deserves to be, although contemporary critics, such as the *New Yorker*'s Richard Brody, continue to champion it. "There's real chemistry between Peck and Bacall, which Minnelli spotlights in carefully observed intimacies and brusque banter alike," Brody wrote. At the time, almost all who reviewed it were unanimous in their praise of Bacall. *Variety* called her "excellent," while the *Los Angeles Valley Times* proclaimed: "This time Lauren Bacall reaches dizzy heights in thespic stature."

It was perhaps her best performance of the 1950s—and, in a way, a bittersweet swansong to her time as a classic leading lady. Her career in movies had never followed an easy trajectory. Aside from her debut, which came with all the praise and success she hadn't been prepared for, the rest had always been a struggle. Now, her biggest ally was gone—as she was soon to find out, losing Bogie meant more than losing a life partner. Her stock in Hollywood, which had been shaky to begin with, would soon plummet. Sure, she had just scored two successful movies and felt like she was on top of her game. But as the press never failed to highlight, she was now "Lauren Bacall, Humphrey Bogart's widow," not "Lauren Bacall, a successful actor." This perception would continue to plague her for the rest of her life—wrestling with the legend of her late husband, and of herself as one half of the "Bogie and his Baby" myth, would become something she'd have to learn to navigate. For now, her wounds were too fresh for her to be able to truly grasp any of that. What she wanted more than anything was to live—a natural response to the months of existing alongside the dark specter of death. She was physically and emotionally exhausted, though there was likely no one to make her aware of it. "I wanted it all to come back," she would write in her memoir. "I wanted to wake up smiling again—I wanted something to look forward to—I hated feeling that my life was over at thirty-two."

In the months following Bogie's death, Sinatra continued to be an important presence in Lauren's life. She spent the days following the funeral at Frank's Palm Springs home, although he was still in New York performing. He called her, offered friendly warmth and the sort of confident positivity she craved. Sometime during that summer, things progressed from friendship to romance. Still grieving and without a chance to truly come to terms with what had happened, and with her raw emotions on full display, Lauren was at her most vulnerable. Sinatra's marriage to Ava Gardner, from whom he'd been separated since 1954, was over, although, as Lauren was to discover, his obsessional love for her continued. The press quickly caught wind of the new relationship, and the pairing of Sinatra and Bacall became a hot topic. Marriage rumors began circulating almost immediately. "She is witty, gay, loyal, and has already proved that her husband's happiness was more important to her than her own career," wrote the columnist James Bacon. The "good wife" material was not exactly a label Lauren cared for, but as her feelings for Frank became more intense, she began to envisage their future together. Promises were made. Frank was telling friends that they'd be married and was excitingly planning the wedding. At the same time, he was emotionally unavailable, with shifting moods and unpredictable swings. "I didn't really know where I stood with Frank," she would later write. By the end of that year, it was over. Frank became furious when news of their planned marriage appeared in the headlines, and he accused Lauren of leaking the information, of trying to put pressure on him. She was hurt and confused. He refused to see her. Many of his Hollywood friends and "yes men" shunned her too, making the humiliation almost unbearable.

It seemed that life was crumbling to pieces all around her. The summer after Bogie's death, Natalie suffered a massive heart attack.

Although she recuperated, the incident shook Lauren to the core. The thought of losing her mother, that constant source of strength and support, terrified her. In September, she went back to work. *The Gift of Love* took Lauren back to Twentieth Century-Fox and reunited her with Jean Negulesco for their third and final collaboration. Robert Stack, fresh off his Oscar nomination for *Written on the Wind*, would be her leading man. On paper, things looked promising, but the weepy melodrama lacked substance, and Lauren's part was weak. Playing a woman slowly dying of an incurable heart condition was no doubt an added challenge for her already fragile psyche, but as ever, her professionalism took over. When the film was released in February of 1958, reviews were mixed, although Lauren's work was praised. "Every so often there comes a movie in which the performance of a single player, though it may not be of the soul-stirring Oscar caliber, makes the audience grateful for having seen the film," wrote one critic. "Such an actress is Lauren Bacall." While it was certainly a positive review, the fact that she was seen as reliable and capable, rather than "Oscar caliber," wasn't exactly the sort of feedback she longed for. Had the film become a box-office hit, things might have turned out differently, but *The Gift of Love* quickly disappeared from theaters, making it apparent that the good streak she had enjoyed with *Written on the Wind* and *Designing Woman* would not continue.

Things would have to change, she felt. She needed to find her own identity, reclaim her life, find out if there were still things worth doing. Hollywood didn't feel like home anymore, especially after the humiliating experience with Frank. She sold the house on Mapleton Drive, and she also had to let *Santana* go. It was a symbolic and emotional parting with the past. In October of 1958, she set out on a trip to Europe with Slim Hawks, the woman who more than a decade before had helped her to find her way in Hollywood. Slim, now divorced from Hawks and newly married to Leland Hayward, was once again on hand to guide Lauren, this time, out of the narrow streets of Beverly Hills and onto the open waters of the world beyond.

CHAPTER 6

Welcome to the Theater

CHANGE IS AS INEVITABLE AS IT IS NECESSARY. AT CERTAIN TIMES, A DRASTIC change is imperative to a person's very survival. By 1958, Lauren Bacall had reached such a point. In the previous eighteen months, she had lost the love of her life, endured a very public humiliation and yet another heartbreak. She saw her career slip down a slippery slope; she lost friends. At thirty-five, she felt lost and finished. Both her self-esteem and her spirits were at an all-time low. One of the most important characteristics of a legend, an enduring star, is their instinctive ability to adapt and evolve, no matter the climate—to survive. It's unlikely that at this point Lauren thought about herself as a legend-in-the-making. She simply followed her desire to live, that strongest of all impulses.

"That trip with (Slim) was the beginning of my being saved," Lauren later wrote. "The first step toward facing and dealing with my life as it truly was—not as I wished it were." After some weeks in Spain and Paris, she arrived in London. She had always loved the city, but now it felt like home. The theatrical elite welcomed her with open arms—not only as Bogie's widow, but as a good friend, and a woman of value and talent of her own. She was able to easily rekindle old acquaintances, which quickly turned into enduring friendships. Vivien Leigh and Laurence Olivier, who had first become friendly with the Bogarts during their 1950 sojourn in Hollywood, where they had been shooting *A Streetcar Named Desire* and *Carrie* respectively, made Lauren feel at home. Their own marriage had reached an end—after two decades of tremendous highs and terrifying lows, Olivier was about to leave Vivien. She was in the middle of a manic phase of her bipolar disorder, insisting on throwing Lauren a huge welcome party, attended by the who's-who of London's theater and film worlds, along with a crowd of journalists. Beyond Leigh's illness, Lauren recognized in Vivien the same attempt to resurface from the depths of despair she herself was going through, and she felt fiercely protective of this beautiful and fragile woman. Along with Kay Kendall, the three formed a close bond: three women against the world.

While in London, Lauren was offered the female lead in *North West Frontier*, an epic story set in British India in 1905, in which she was to play a spunky American governess of an Indian prince, on the run from a violent Muslim uprising. It was the first role offered to her since *The Gift of Love*. Hollywood had all but given up on her, at least that's how it felt, and she was happy at the prospect of starring in a prestige British production. Filming was due to start in the spring of 1959, giving her time to go back to the States and make the necessary arrangements for her Hollywood exodus. "There comes a time when you've been in the same place for too long," she told the press. "You start to forget about the rest of the world. It's time I went out to find out what's going on elsewhere."

Lauren, Stephen, and Leslie arrived in London in January 1959, where Lauren rented a large flat in Cadogan Place, an exclusive address in Kensington, and she enrolled the children at the American School. The cold English winter must have been a shock to the youngsters, especially after the balmy climate of California, but there was much fun to be had in this new city. The London Zoo was a particular favorite, and then there were the museums, the red buses, the theater. Lauren felt reinvigorated, filled with a new sense of optimism for the future. She wasn't sure what awaited, but for the first time in months she allowed herself to think that whatever it was, it would be good.

In April, she left for India to start shooting. Arriving in this new country, full of vibrant colors, unfamiliar noises, and vast crowds of people, jolted her back to life more than anything she could have experienced back home. Few people knew or cared who she was—here, she was just another foreigner, an anonymous white woman wandering the busy bazaars, overflowing with exotic spices and shiny jewels. *North West Frontier* was mainly being shot in and around Jaipur, where the cast crew stayed at an impressive hotel, once the residence of the Maharajah. The British company treated Lauren like a star, and she enjoyed it. Her Hollywood glamour was appreciated here much more than it had been back home. In Los Angeles, she was just one of many movie queens, but here, she was The Star. Kenneth More, the popular English leading man of the 1950s, who was playing the movie's hero, Captain Scott, was among those under Bacall's sultry spell. In his memoir, he admitted to thinking she was "one of the most desirable women in the world," and although married at the time, he frankly writes about having fantasies of seducing Bacall once on location. The affair wasn't to be, Lauren apparently not returning More's affections, although the two did enjoy a platonic trip to visit the Taj Mahal during a break in shooting. The sweltering heat was at times unbearable. The papers back in London reported with delight that the American star "needs constant run downs with ice and even takes ice to bed with her at night." The situation wasn't made easy by the period costumes she was required to wear in the film: a heavy full-length skirt, four petticoats, white wool stockings, wool cloak, and a giant hood. Many members of the crew were taken ill, while Lauren herself was reported to have fainted while shooting the mob scenes. "She just went down in the dust, in the middle of the crowd," director Lee Thompson told journalists. "She's a really strong personality and doesn't mind what she's being asked to do. She'd hate you to know what happened, but I can tell you she was really frightened, and so was I."

Lauren's part in *North West Frontier* once again lacks the depth and scope to show off her range and versatility as an actor. The character of Catherine Wyatt is paper-thin, with only a few short moments where Bacall's able to hint at what she's capable of. One such sequence is the scene in which Catherine insists on personally going through a train, full of massacred bodies, searching for any survivors. The scene is perhaps the most memorable of the entire movie, and Lauren manages to convey an array of emotions without a single line of dialogue. When she finally emerges from the last carriage, with a newborn infant in her arms, the camera focuses on her face in what is one of the most beautiful close-ups of Bacall's career: she is a Madonna, the ultimate feminine figure, the one to bring the hope of a new life, even amid death and darkness. Considering the timing, it's hard not to view the scene as deeply symbolic and meaningful for Bacall herself—the triumph of life over death, a rebirth.

The train sequence was filmed in the Granada region of Spain, where the company moved to in May. The sparse Spanish landscape stood in for the plains of India for the remainder of the shoot, making it easy for Lauren to visit Malaga, where she was introduced to Ernest Hemingway. Papa had been a fan of Bacall's ever since seeing her in *To Have and Have Not*. While he thought little of the film itself, the young actress had impressed him greatly. Always an admirer of Bogart, Hemingway was impressed by the stories he'd heard of Lauren's bravery in the face of her husband's illness. She was, in many ways, the kind of woman who could have easily been part of his literary world.

After some additional interior shots were completed in England, the filming of *North West Frontier* wrapped in the summer of 1959. When the film was released that fall, it became a huge hit in the UK, where the press reviewed it enthusiastically. It was an epic on a scale not seen since the heyday of Alexander Korda, and the thinly veiled pro-Empire sentiment was welcomed by British audiences. In the States, the film was largely overlooked, and it did little to change Lauren's standing in Hollywood. Neither was she keen to go back to California anytime soon. Had she stayed in London, she might have been offered more work in British films, and the prospect was tempting. But something else presented itself during these months in Europe which was hard to pass on. The theater. Her girlhood dream of having her name in lights on a Broadway marquee. It also meant the relative security of steady employment (although, as she would soon learn, nothing is secure in the world of the theater). So, she packed up her bags, took the children out of the American School, bade farewell to her London friends, said a tearful goodbye to Slim Hawks, and boarded a plane back home. New York, New York.

• • •

The script for George Axelrod's latest play, *Goodbye Charlie*, had been given to Lauren by Leland Hayward while she was in Spain with him and Slim the previous year. She read it and found it funny—her part was challenging, perhaps the most difficult thing she'd ever been asked to do, at least up to that point. Axelrod was a good friend, once telling her that should she ever decide to try stage, it ought to be in one of his plays. He also told her that the role of Charlie had been written with her in mind—a gift few actors can resist. And so here she was—back in New York, the city where it all began, ready to start rehearsals for her first starring role on Broadway.

Goodbye Charlie contained some of Axelrod's signature double entendre and a rather risqué play on the traditional gender roles—in many ways, the play was ahead of its time, making it unpalatable for many audiences (and critics) in the America of 1959. For Lauren to tackle the role of a man reincarnated as a woman was also seen as a brave move—or a foolish one. She saw it only as a challenge. The idea of gender reversal was to her mind "far-out," but also "creative and funny." It's unlikely that she would ever have been given a similar opportunity in movies. By the end of the 1950s, most of her film noir sisters had found themselves struggling to maintain steady employment in Hollywood. Even the most successful, like Ava Gardner and Rita Hayworth, were already being seen as relics of a bygone era (Gardner was thirty-eight in 1960, Hayworth forty-two). Lauren was barely thirty-six, and not nearly ready to hang up her gloves. As an actress, and as a woman, she felt as though she was just beginning.

"For the first time in my adult life I began to call on all my resources as an actress, to really use myself," she would write about the weeks of work on her part in *Goodbye Charlie*. Axelrod was making his debut as a director, which sometimes made things complicated. The actors found it difficult to speak frankly to him about any faults in the play, and he in turn was reluctant to make changes to his own writing. For Lauren, it was all new—she had to learn how to project her voice, how to move on stage, how to preserve her energy and stay in character for the entire duration of the play, rather than for a movie take. As she had done with Hawks all those years before, she now placed all her trust in Axelrod and Hayward. "For a woman of strong opinions, supposedly outspoken and in control, it's odd that I was quite prepared to do things almost entirely their way, to more or less turn myself over to them," she reflected later.

Sydney Chaplin, who had been cast as her male costar, proved to be of enormous help. Significantly more experienced as a theater actor, Chaplin was generous and friendly, and Lauren was grateful to have him as a partner. After an intense rehearsal period, the company went on tour—the idea was to get the actors, and Lauren in particular, used to the play and the live audience, before the hype of Broadway and New York's critics. There had been great anticipation in Pittsburgh, Pennsylvania, where the play was to open on October 19, 1959. Lauren Bacall, the great movie star, the widow of Humphrey Bogart was to make her much-talked-about stage debut (the fact she had done theater before Hollywood was seldom mentioned in the press). Lauren later remembered shaking throughout the entirety of the opening night. It was a nerve-wracking, terrifying, and utterly exhilarating experience. After the house lights came on, the roar of applause hit the stage and, as she later wrote, "from that night on I was to be forever hooked on the theater." Pittsburgh critics were puzzled by the play, with most reviews less than generous to Axelrod's writing and direction, but all praised Lauren. "Ms. Bacall is a sound actress with all the right instincts," wrote one critic, adding that "she is working here at close and hollow quarters, which are as yet confiding and unrewarding." The same review stated that "Mr. Hayward has given *Goodbye Charlie* a lush, tasteful production but right now it merely houses the shell of a play Mr. Axelrod will have to be something of a miracle man to fill."

It was a trend which persisted for the remainder of the play's run. By the time the show reached Broadway in December, Axelrod had made significant changes in the script, including the play's final scene. Unfortunately, his efforts weren't enough to save the production. New York's critics were savage to him, although they largely spared his actors. Lauren's star power meant that ticket sales were strong, making the show a moderate success, despite the mixed critical reception. She could certainly be proud of herself. She had done it—she was a Broadway star.

Many of her New York reviews were indeed raves, though she was likely too disappointed for Axelrod and the overall reception of the play to fully appreciate her achievement. "Ms. Bacall plays the newly-sexed Charlie with humor and great charm," proclaimed John Chapman of the *Daily News*, while the *New York Times*' Brooks Atkinson felt she played the part like "a cross between a female impersonator and Tallulah Bankhead." For any readers in doubt whether the remark was meant as a compliment, Atkinson went to state that Bacall "can take satisfaction in realizing that she is playing it as well as anyone could, Lon Chaney and Mae West not excepted." Lauren's talent for comedy and high camp was at long last being utilized, although, it would take another few years before she'd get the chance to fully develop and showcase these skills again.

Goodbye Charlie closed in March of 1960, after less than three months—much less than the year everyone had hoped for. Lauren worried that her friendship with Axelrod had suffered and that she hadn't done enough to ensure that play's success. It was a difficult time—suspended somewhere between Hollywood and Broadway, not fully belonging to either, she now felt as though both worlds viewed her with suspicion. In the midst of what was already an emotionally loaded time, she had also fallen in love.

Jason Robards was an esteemed stage actor, a serious intellectual, a brooding, handsome man, with more than a passing resemblance to

Bogie—a fact noticed by everyone, especially the press. He was also married. Despite this, they began seeing each other while they were both starring in different Broadway plays: Lauren in *Charlie*, Robards in *Toys in the Attic*. The romance seemed like a consummation of Lauren's transition into her New York life since no one was more New York than Jason. After their respective shows, they'd venture into the Greenwich Village nights, visiting bars and bohemian hangouts Lauren had no idea existed. She was introduced to real actors, not merely movie stars: Maureen Stapleton, Eli Wallach, Geraldine Page, Ben Gazzara, and the almighty Strasbergs. She was dazzled, wanted to be part of it all. "I wasn't truly one of them, but they let me in nonetheless, and I was deeply grateful," she later wrote. By late summer of 1960, the press caught wind of the affair. "The Lauren Bacall–Jason Robards palship causes fireworks!" announced Earl Wilson in his column. They were suddenly the hot new item, the last thing either of them wanted. Lauren was appalled at some of the journalists who used their pieces to wonder how Robards would compare to Bogie, could he fill the late actor's shoes? Others noted bitingly that the romance helped ticket sales for *Toys in the Attic* improve significantly. If Jason's career benefited from the attention, Lauren's did not. She had hoped that after *Goodbye Charlie* other offers of stage work would follow, but for the time being, she remained unemployed.

From the start, their relationship was volatile. Robards was prone to depression and rapidly changing moods. He also drank, a fact that friends had warned her about and she chose to ignore. She was desperate to rebuild her life, and in her mind, that meant a home and a man. She also felt that the children needed a father figure, and both Leslie and especially Stephen immediately loved Jason. Robards's wife, Rachel Taylor, filed for divorce citing Lauren as the cause—although in private the two women got on well. Robards already had three children, and they soon became a blended family, with Lauren subletting a huge apartment in the famed Dakota building on the western edge of Central Park. The place was big enough for everyone, and it had both grandeur and privacy—luxuries taken for granted in Los Angeles but rare in Manhattan.

In the spring of 1961, Lauren discovered she was pregnant. She wanted this baby, she wanted Jason. He was alternating between desperately clinging to her and pushing her away, a familiar pattern which should have set off alarm bells. Some of her old friends seemed to distance themselves from Lauren, feeling that her relationship with Robards was toxic. They traveled to Europe, where Robards was to appear in the film version of *Tender Is the Night,* and although things should have been blissful, Lauren spent most of the time alone and miserable. In her memoir, she admits contemplating abortion, although her desire to keep the baby outweighed her doubts about the future with Jason. There were few happy reunions—she didn't see Slim Hawks, and while in London, she didn't introduce Robards to Vivien Leigh or to Olivier (who was by now married to Joan Plowright).

They planned to get married in Vienna, a city Lauren had never seen before, far away from friends and family. Lauren recalled the unhappy experience of being asked to produce her late husband's death certificate on the spot. "Surely you know he's dead," she responded in shock. "Every newspaper in the world headlined his death." Apparently, that wasn't enough to satisfy the local bureaucracy. In addition, proof of Robards's divorce papers was also needed. The marriage could not take place—a bad omen, and one that would follow them to Las Vegas, where due to a legality concerning the necessary wait time between a Mexican divorce and a Nevada wedding, they were once again denied a marriage license. In the end, they flew to Mexico, where they were finally pronounced man and wife on July 4, 1961. The ceremony was in Spanish, and Lauren did not understand a word of it. All she knew was that she was now Mrs. Jason Robards.

***

Married life was anything but smooth. Lauren desperately wanted things to work out. She loved Jason deeply, or at least, the version of him she allowed herself to see. His drinking and unpredictability were often too much to swallow, and she found herself depressed and constantly worried, a far from an ideal state for a new wife and soon-to-be mother. Prospects of work were few—once again, Lauren's desire to please her man, which stood in such contrast with her independent spirit, meant that, for a time, her professional ambition was to take a back seat.

Their son was born on December 16, 1961. They named him Sam—just Sam, not Samuel. It was love at first sight for Lauren. Whatever problems she was facing with Jason, she would never regret her decision to have this baby. Robards continued his rise up the ladder of theatrical success, with acclaimed performances in *A Thousand Clowns* during the 1962–63 season and in Arthur Miller's controversial play, *After the Fall*, which was staged by the newly formed, short-lived Repertory Theatre of Lincoln Center in 1964. Lauren longed for more stage glory too, but the offers failed to come. Her marriage too gave her little happiness. Most evenings she sat in their huge Dakota apartment, waiting for Jason to come home after his performance, but more often than not, he'd go out drinking instead. The strain of never knowing where he was and when he'd be home impacted her emotional and physical health. She was thinner than ever, chain-smoking, feeling trapped but reluctant to admit, even to herself, that she'd made a mistake.

By 1964, she was ready to accept almost any work that came her way. With no stage prospects in New York, she turned to Hollywood. Since she had departed some five years earlier, it seemed no one there missed her. Or at least, none of the people responsible for casting. She received some offers for TV series, which she turned down. Her comeback to the screen would be a leading role in *Shock Treatment*, a poorly written thriller, set to capitalize on the recent success of psycho-biddy horrors like *What Ever Happened to Baby Jane* and *Hush . . . Hush, Sweet Charlotte*, with elements of *Psycho* thrown in. While hardly a quality project, her part was surprisingly complex. Dr. Edwina Beighley is a psychiatrist, an ambitious career woman, who gradually reveals herself as a greedy sadist and ends up losing her mind. Lauren approached the work with the same dedication she would have had it been Tennessee Williams or Shakespeare. So what if the movie was a stinker—she would show them all that she still had it. For the most part, watching Bacall in the film is a pleasure. Her transformation is slow and unsettling. There's also a new confidence in her acting, no doubt a result of her theater experience, but also her exposure to the New York actors she had gotten to know since her move East. Giving a quality performance, no matter how mediocre the material, was a mark of a true actor. An actor had to work—and no part was too small, no project too insignificant. That's what distinguished real actors from movie stars, and Lauren wanted nothing more than to be regarded as the former. This New York-style approach to work would become her philosophy: as long as she was able to work, she was developing her craft, expanding, using herself. It was no use waiting for some glamorous star vehicle to magically present itself. She was no Norma Desmond; she was a working actor.

Bacall's character in *Shock Treatment* is eerily similar to that of Nurse Ratched from *One Flew Over the Cuckoo's Nest* (the novel upon which *Shock Treatment* was based had been published in 1961, a year before Ken Kesey's *Cuckoo's Nest*), making one wonder what Bacall could have achieved had she been offered better material. Unfortunately, when Milos Forman made *Cuckoo's Nest* into a film in 1975, Lauren wasn't considered for the part.

Shock Treatment was panned by critics, and it sank at the box office. Lauren saw it as an embarrassment, and along with *Confidential Agent*, as the worst thing she'd ever done, the lowest point in her career. The fact that many reviewers singled her out for praise was of little consolation. "In all this confusion (of the plot), a few compensations manage to survive," stated one critic. "Lauren Bacall as the psychiatrist, in particular, turns in a performance that is creditable. Her evolution from dedicated professional to sadistic schemer is the thread that holds the picture together and nothing less than the quality of her acting could have made this possible."

For Lauren, the one high point of doing the film was a chance to reestablish her friendship with Roddy McDowall, who played the Norman Bates-like character of a psychopathic gardener. They enjoyed each other's company, and Lauren was happy to be inducted into Roddy's inner circle. Home movies shot by McDowall in his Malibu beach house show Lauren mingling and joking around with some of the biggest names in the movie business, many of whom represented the "New Hollywood," including Natalie Wood, Jane Fonda, Anthony Perkins. Older friends, like Judy Garland, would also drop by. These were fleeting moments of happiness during an otherwise miserable time. While she loved Roddy and enjoyed meeting his friends, she didn't feel like she belonged in this Hollywood. Perhaps she had never really belonged here at all? As long as Bogie had been alive, things were different. Now, the old charm had all but evaporated. The few treasured friends she still had there were always a joy to see, particularly Hepburn and Tracy. But despite the sun and ocean, which she loved, without Bogie, California would never feel like home again.

However, for better or worse, this was the place where the work was. Soon after completing *Shock Treatment,* Lauren was offered a supporting role in the comedy *Sex and the Single Girl,* which was to star Natalie Wood and Tony Curtis, with Lauren's old friend and *Petrified Forest* costar, Henry Fonda, playing her husband. Once again, she had reservations about the script, and she wasn't too happy about playing second fiddle to Natalie Wood, then at the height of her fame, and her beauty. Bacall's character, Sylvia, a jealous wife with a hot temper, gets a lot of the movie's laughs, and Lauren takes every little opportunity to make the most out of her screen time. Once again, paired with the much older Fonda and dressed in matron-y costumes which stand in sharp contrast with Wood's sexy wardrobe, Lauren is made to appear older than her thirty-nine years. The film, inspired by the bestselling nonfiction book of the same title, was at the time seen as bold, if silly, in its approach to the subject of sex. By appearing in it, Lauren crossed over to the swinging sixties—it was a move that proved difficult for many stars of the classical era. She managed to exist both as a modern celebrity and an old-time movie star, a juggling act she would maintain for the rest of her life.

When *Sex and the Single Girl* came out on Christmas Day of 1964, it became a big hit with audiences, making it one of the top moneymakers of the year. Reviews were mostly mixed, criticizing the script for its shallowness, but Lauren was happy to have an unexpected hit on her hands. Making the film in Hollywood, on the Warners Burbank lot, twenty years after she had first stepped onto the same sound stage to make *To Have and Have Not* with Bogie, was something of a bittersweet homecoming. She couldn't help but notice how much the industry had changed. There was no more of the talent-nurturing or star-curating that had gone on in the old days. But the legend of Bogie and Bacall was still very much part of the town's lore, a fact which filled her with a mixture of emotions—pride on the one hand, and on the other, fear of getting frozen in the iconography of the past instead of being regarded as an active, working actor.

Her next film, which also proved to be her last of the 1960s, would only confirm this duality of her screen image. *Harper*, based on the 1949 detective novel *The Moving Target*, would mark the beginning of postclassical cinema's cult of Bogie, as well as a part of the new generation's attempt to recreate the mystique of film noir. While the actual academic definition of film noir as a style of filmmaking wouldn't be widely used until the 1970s, by the 1960s, the movies and the stars from the 1940s were already considered iconic, and Bogart, perhaps the most iconic of all.

In *Harper*, the part of the Bogart-esque private eye is played by Paul Newman, who is sexy and cool as only Newman can be, but the essence of the character is very much the same as Bogie's Philip Marlowe: cynical, unlucky in love, wisecracking, and despite the veneer of indifference, deeply committed to doing the right thing. Lauren's part in the film is significantly smaller than in any of her original film noir projects, and it's quite clear that her presence is used to create a vital connection with Bogart. Despite those limitations, she manages to create a full-bodied performance, escaping becoming nothing more than a glamorous cameo. She was wary of accepting the role, especially given the problems in her marriage to Robards. What's more, the renewed public fascination with Bogie was bound to create even more tension. She knew that she'd be forever bound to Bogart, but by choosing to appear in *Harper*, she symbolically made peace with it.

For all its references to classic Hollywood, *Harper* is also a quintessentially '60s movie, with a psychedelic color pallet, swinging dancers, and beaded cult leaders. Lauren approached her character as a contemporary woman; she didn't want to see her as a throwback to her noir days. She was tired of journalists asking her to repeat the "just whistle" line. "Just when I thought even the nightclub comics were forgetting it, TV revived the movie and it started haunting me again," she complained. When *Harper* came out, it became a hit with both critics and audiences. Reviews of Bacall's work were complimentary, with some choosing her as the highlight of the film, despite her limited screen time and an impressive ensemble, which also included Julie Harris, Shelley Winters, Arthur Hill, and Robert Wagner. "It's the calm and collected Miss Bacall who walks away with the picture," stated Herb Kelly of the *Miami News*. "She's like a cat—sly and unpredictable." Other critics also pointed out the catlike quality: "Miss Bacall is her usual sharp-clawed feline," wrote Bosley Crowther. Some of the articles were bound to leave Jason less than happy:

"When you look at Lauren Bacall, you think of Humphrey Bogart," Kelly opened his review, while another critic asked, "After all, who on earth could measure up to Bogart?" While the rhetorical question was aimed at Paul Newman, it must have been hard for Lauren Bacall's current husband to read it and not apply it to himself.

CHAPTER 7

A Star Is Reborn

THE SUCCESS OF *HARPER* DID LITTLE TO REESTABLISH LAUREN'S STANDING IN Hollywood. The fact that she had two hit movies in a row meant little, as she wasn't seen as the main draw in either of them even if her reviews were glowing. She was tired of trying to prove herself to movie producers, of convincing skeptics that she was a capable actor. Hell, if after nearly two decades in the business they still didn't think so, maybe they never would.

For a time, she stayed in her rented Malibu home with little Sam, gathering thoughts, occasionally seeing old friends, taking walks on the beach. With no movie offers, and the future of her marriage uncertain, she felt like she was drifting, not at all sure of where she was heading. For all the confidence and bravura her public persona exuded, privately Bacall was a highly sensitive, anxious person. "I've lived with one anxiety or another my entire life," she reflected in *Now*. "While Bogie was alive, I had him to boost me, help me through the rough times. After Bogie, I had mostly me, and the memory of him."

Once again, it was the theater which helped to get her through rough times. While she was still on the West Coast, Abe Burrows sent her the script for a play entitled *Cactus Flower*. It was a delicious comedy, adapted from a French farce by Burrows himself, with a great part for Lauren.

Burrows wanted her—it wasn't a matter of having to convince anyone that she was right for the part, as had so often been the case in movies. "I felt I had value for the play and was wanted by the producers and the director, not as though they were doing me a favor," she later wrote.

She was to play a shy yet witty, spinsterish nurse in a dental office, secretly in love with her boss who, in turn, chases after a younger woman, to whom he pretends to be married to Lauren's character in order to avoid commitment. It was pure comic delight, and Lauren would be called on to use all the skills previous film roles had only partially allowed her to showcase. Timing would be everything. As soon as rehearsals were underway in New York, she realized she would have some tough competition. Brenda Vaccaro, the young Italian American actress cast as the bubbly love interest, had some of the play's funniest lines, as well as a natural comedic talent with the potential to steal the show. While Lauren never publicly spoke or wrote about her insecurity, Vaccaro later recalled Burrows asking her to tone down her performance, which she refused to do. "I don't know where my audacity came from," she told William J. Mann in 2020. "I could have lost my job." It isn't clear if Lauren had anything to do with Burrows's request—for the entire run, she would never be anything but polite and professional with her younger colleague.

It's hardly surprising Bacall felt a great deal of pressure; she was carrying the show on her shoulders, with her name and image alone on all the promotional materials and posters. After the first preview in Washington, the play's leading man, Joe Campanella, was replaced by the more experienced Barry Nelson. Lauren felt bad for Campanella but had to admit that her performance, and the entire show, improved with Nelson. By the time they reached Broadway on December 8, 1965, it was obvious the company had a hit on their hands. Reviews were uniformly enthusiastic, with Lauren finally getting the recognition she had longed for. "Thanks to the rare comic touch of Lauren Bacall, *Cactus Flower* is one of the few non-musicals entering Broadway's summer doldrums with heavy bookings for next season," announced the press. Lauren was ecstatic, reveling in her success.

"You can't do much better than that," she told a journalist while relaxing in her Dakota apartment's library. "Movies made proper use of me at first, but after I fell out of Howard Hawks's hands, I went into a survival period. Now things are opening up for me. After years of work that didn't satisfy, I've suddenly stirred up a lot of interest again."

Lauren would stay in *Cactus Flower* for two years—an enormous challenge for her, both physically and mentally. The show continued to bring in crowds, and Lauren remained the toast of the town. By contrast, home life was anything but happy. Just as Lauren was enjoying her success, Jason's play, *The Devils,* turned out to be a failure, causing him to drink even more than before. This time, she refused to let anything stand in the way of her own professional triumph. The boost which came from the show helped her to assert herself, to face up to reality. Her marriage wasn't going to work, and it was alright. For the first time in a long while, she believed she could make it on her own. The final break up came in 1968 after Lauren discovered Robards's short-lived affair. In truth, the marriage had been over for a long time, but the affair seemed like a good time to finally end it, for both their sakes. She walked away from the relationship bruised but strong. Other blows were harder to deal with. Throughout the 1960s, some of the most important people in her life passed away: Adlai Stevenson in 1965, followed by Spencer Tracy and Vivien Leigh in 1967. Then, in August of 1969, Lauren's beloved mother died from a heart attack. Natalie was only sixty-nine, and her loss was profound. She had always been a rock, the one constant source of support. Through all the pain, Lauren felt herself entering a new era: a time of independence, of learning what it meant to be alone. Work, friendships, children—she would now dedicate herself to all of it. There was no man to live for anymore, and no mother figure to guide her. She was by herself.

The enormous success of *Cactus Flower* on stage meant that inevitably a film version would follow. Lauren's reviews had been glowing, she had carried the hit production on her shoulders for two years. And yet, she was careful not to take being cast in the movie for granted, especially given her track record with Hollywood producers. Not too long before, Audrey Hepburn so infamously walked away with the role of Eliza Doolittle in the film of *My Fair Lady*, after Julie Andrews's star-making turn in the role on Broadway. Filmdom's politics were baffling to Lauren, even after all these years. She wanted to do the film more than she had any other in a long time. She knew she was good in the part, and she also felt that it would showcase her versatility and comic ability more than any of the roles she had played onscreen up to then. In the end, after being promised the part, and after her agent had announced publicly that she had been cast, the producers gave the role to Ingrid Bergman instead. It was a shocking and curious turn of events. Bergman might have had two Oscars under her belt, but by 1968 she was hardly considered a box-office pull. Unlike Bacall, she had never done comedy before and was far from an obvious choice for the part. To Lauren, it was further proof that Hollywood had it in for her. She couldn't help but feel victimized, especially since the disappointing blow came at the same time as the profound losses in her personal life.

Publicly, she would always be careful not to speak out against Bergman; the two had shared a warm, if casual, relationship over the years. They were, for better or worse, two of Bogie's most iconic costars. In fact, the resurgence of *Casablanca*'s popularity might have accounted for Hollywood's renewed interest in Bergman. Woody Allen's *Play It Again, Sam* opened on Broadway in February 1969 and became an instant hit, propelling Bogart to new heights of iconography. He was seen as the ultimate symbol of cool, the godfather to the Steve McQueens and the Paul Newmans. Both Bergman and Lauren benefited from this by proxy, but while Bergman had always enjoyed the reputation as a serious actor, for Bacall it was considerably harder to break away from the "Bogie's Baby" mold. In the end, it was the newcomer, Goldie Hawn, who'd prove herself the real star of the film version of *Cactus*, walking away with an Oscar for best supporting actress. For Lauren, the disappointment pushed her into a state of depression. "That's the way it goes, or that's the way it went," she'd later write about the episode. "Your day will come, I kept telling myself."

Her day came a few months later, in the early summer of 1969, when she was approached about starring in the stage musical version of the 1950 classic film, *All About Eve*—one of her heroine Bette Davis's most iconic roles. The book wasn't ready, the score only partially composed—and yet, she had no doubt that it was the role and the challenge of a lifetime, and one she could not turn down. There were plenty of reasons to feel apprehensive. She had never done a musical before, she was certainly not a singer, and the role was already made so iconic by Davis that anyone else tackling it would inevitably face added scrutiny. But, in true Bacall fashion, throwing caution to the wind, she accepted the challenge.

The casting was announced by the *New York Times* on July 10. She flew to Europe for a short holiday, loaded with the tapes of songs she was to learn and ready to start the vocal exercises she had been shown by her coach. Money was short as she hadn't worked in months, but old friends came through, as ever. She spent time with David Niven and his wife in their beautiful villa in Cap Ferret, on the Atlantic coast of France. Niven would find her belting out her songs into the open ocean, joking that she sounded like a seal calling for a mate. Then it was to London and more friends; Vivien Leigh had passed away back in 1967, and it was strange not to see her lovely face upon arrival, but there were still others Lauren was happy to see. The city would always hold a special place in her heart.

Rehearsals for the play, now titled *Applause,* started in November, just two months after the death of Lauren's mother. She was still fragile, still grieving the loss, as well as the end of her marriage. But the all-encompassing rigors of musical theater proved the best possible remedy. "I had never worked so hard—used so much of myself in mind and body," she later wrote. "It required discipline and stamina." She had more of both than anyone, including herself, had thought possible. Overcoming shyness and insecurity about her vocal limitations, she worked tirelessly to improve. She'd put Sam to bed each evening and lock herself in the library, learning her lines aloud, singing all the songs, practicing late into the night, sometimes with Leslie feeding her the other actors' lines. It was a project she felt she couldn't afford to fail in; every waking moment was consumed by thinking about or working on the play.

Besides the technical challenges of performing the musical numbers, Lauren found the character of Margo Channing to be the perfect fit for her, particularly at this stage of her life. Since Twentieth Century-Fox had declined to let the producers use the Mankiewicz film script, the book, written by Bacall's friends Betty Comden and Adolph Green, was instead based on the original 1946 *Cosmopolitan* story, "The Wisdom of Eve," which had inspired the film. This meant that Margo's zingiest lines, so endlessly quoted by female impersonators and movie fans, would be absent from the play. It was a blessing in disguise because Lauren wouldn't have to compete with Davis, at least not directly. Her Margo would be different; where Davis had been bitchy and flawlessly witty, Bacall would instead showcase the character's vulnerability and desperation. This contrasting juxtaposition of qualities, ranging from exuberant self-confidence in public to crippling self-doubt in private, would constitute the very foundation of Bacall's performance. Perhaps without fully realizing it, she had made Margo Channing her own creation, remaking her in her own image, rather than using Davis as a model. She had never before so fully used herself in creating a character, never bared herself so completely before an audience—either in the theater or in film.

Applause premiered at the Palace Theatre on March 30, 1970, after some weeks of previews in Detroit and Baltimore. After the opening night, the company gathered at Sardi's to await the reviews—per sacred tradition, this hotspot of New York's theaterland would be the first to get the morning papers.

"Miss Bacall is a sensation," declared Clive Barnes of the *New York Times*. "Whatever it is Miss Lauren Bacall possesses, she throws it around most beautifully, most exquisitely, and most excitingly in a musical called *Applause*."

Others were just as enthusiastic. "Miss Bacall is the most stylish, natural and enchanting dynamo I have recently seen walking, dancing, singing, and acting," raved another. She was called "remarkable" and "splendid." Critics predicted that the show (and Bacall in it) would be around for a long time. A few days later, another review appeared in the *Times*, this one by Walter Kerr, which went even further in its praise. The piece, aptly titled "Bacall Takes Your Breath Away," went on to state that "Miss Bacall sidesteps nothing. Narrowing her eyes until they glitter as dirtily as a sharp piece of glass on a lawn you're roaming barefoot, roaring out her rage with the impassioned hurt of a spoiled child, springing into abandoned dance to express everything from foolish benevolence to fasten-your-seatbelts fury, she is Medea, Medusa and Theda Bara combined and dyed blond. Take your breath away? Indeed. What's more, she never gives it back."

The show was a smash—not since *To Have and Have Not* had Lauren experienced such a high, only this time, it felt even sweeter. She was on top of the world. Her biggest childhood dream had come true—she was a bona fide star in a Broadway musical.

Lauren's success in *Applause* reminded the world of her existence, as well as her potential. She had been right there all along, and yet her talent had been largely neglected and unutilized. "We can't understand why Miss Bacall has remained in comparative obscurity these last few years," wondered one critic, stating that she had been "in eclipse for much too long." She was by no means alone in her struggle to remain visible and active. By the dawn of the 1970s, virtually all female stars of her generation had faded from the screen's firmament. In most cases, they were forced to retire or seek other avenues for their talent. Bacall's spectacular reinvention is a testament to her perseverance and determination—her transition from a dwindling movie career to a stellar one on stage remains a rare trick. *Applause* would prove the perfect vehicle to serve this purpose—at once referencing one of the most pivotal achievements of classical Hollywood and adding to it the cultural flavor of the moment, the show utilized Bacall's glamorous past while also allowing her to show that she was relevant and current. She was no relic of the past—she *was* the moment.

Only a day after the show officially opened, Tony nominations were announced. *Applause* earned a record eleven nods, with two best supporting actress nominations. Lauren was up for best actress in a musical, against competition from her dear friend Katharine Hepburn, who had also made her musical debut in *Coco* the past December, and Dilys Watling in *Georgie*. It was the first major industry award she had ever been up for, and she desperately wanted to win, although being up against Hepburn made it awkward to openly admit just how much the win would mean to her. In her private correspondence with Hepburn, Lauren was gracious and modest, downplaying the importance of the honor and predicting her friend's victory.

Less than a month later, on the evening of April 19, as Walter Matthau announced Bacall as the winner, there was no more modesty or bashfulness, only pure joy as she shot up to the stage to collect the trophy. It might have been the happiest night of her life—at least, her professional life. The heartbreak and disappointment of the past fourteen years seemed to have been erased in one magical instant. She closed the ceremony with a dazzling performance of "Welcome to the Theatre," one of the songs from *Applause,* which that night had also been named the best musical of the year. She exuded confidence and star power, even if her voice bore signs of strain from the months of hard work and the excitement of the evening. She wore a sparkling black gown—curiously similar to the one from *To Have and Have Not*—and she looked more beautiful than she had in a long time. That night, she wasn't Bogie's widow, or his Baby, or the "you-know-how-to-whistle" girl. She was Lauren Bacall, the winner.

'I feel, for the first time in my life, that I am accepted for the woman I am, myself," she later told a journalist. "It came at a time in life when I needed it. I earned it. And I intend to fight for it."

She had agreed to stay in the play for just over a year—after the experience of playing *Cactus Flower* for two years straight, she knew a year on Broadway was more than enough. It was a year of hard work, of complete dedication to the theater. The line between the reality of the play and the life outside it was becoming increasingly blurred. Where did Margo Channing end and Lauren Bacall begin?

"She had never done a musical before and she was terribly nervous," recalls her leading man, Len Cariou, who in playing Bill Sampson was also making his musical debut. "But she had the goods. She didn't have the best singing voice, by any means. But she had great star power and was very charismatic. It was a great pleasure to be with her. So good a pleasure that we ended up in bed together."

The romance between Margo and Bill was short-lived. Cariou was fifteen years Lauren's junior, which, as she pointed out during an interview with Charlie Rose many years later, wouldn't have posed as much of a problem had the roles been reversed. They nonetheless managed to stay on friendly terms—neither pretended the relationship had been anything more than it was, even if Lauren's emotional involvement had been deeper than his. She came to depend on him, in the play and outside of it, and was thrown off balance when Cariou left the play early to appear in another production.

One night, the original Margo Channing came to see the play. To have Bette Davis in the audience meant more to Lauren than she could have expressed. To think of little Betty Persky, the usherette who idolized Davis and dreamt of having her own name in lights, now actually performing for Bette Davis, playing the part Davis had made so iconic, seemed like some fantastical cosmic joke. After the show, Lauren waited in her dressing room with a beating heart. There was a knock on the door—and there she stood, all five foot, three inches of her, larger than life. The meeting was short, both women feeling awkward, not having enough time to express how either truly felt. As she was leaving, Davis turned around and looked at Bacall: "No one but you could have played this part—and you know I mean it."

"There was so much more I had wanted to say to her," Lauren later wrote in her memoir. "If we'd had fifteen minutes it might have been warmer, I might have made her realize how much her being there had meant." It is more than likely that Davis would read Bacall's words when *By Myself* was released in 1978, as well as see her gushing over her idol during televised interviews, including on Johnny Carson in 1983.

After the sixteen months of her Broadway triumph was over, Lauren agreed to take the show on the road, heading a national tour, which ended in Los Angeles. She was happy to "show them" that she was a success, that she didn't need "them" and their movies to be a star. But "they," whoever "they" were, paid little attention—theater was not an LA medium. Those who had loved and supported her all along came to see the show, but she did not exactly return with a vengeance in the way she had imagined.

Taking *Applause* to London would prove a happier experience. It was the first time she was to appear on the West End stage, which meant a great deal to her. As ever, she was welcomed by her London friends with open arms and felt right at home. Sam, now almost eleven, accompanied her. Leslie was attending school back in New York. Stephen had married back in 1969, and he and his wife, Dale, welcomed their son Jamie into the world in April of 1970, making Lauren a grandmother at forty-six.

Leaving her New York life behind and establishing a temporary home in London felt like a new start, even if she was still playing Margo. The British critics weren't as forgiving about the shortcomings of the play as their New York colleagues, noticing its tired attitudes towards relationships and women. Margo's opinion that a woman is not a woman unless she can look up in the morning and see a man sleeping next to her might have sounded perfectly palatable when Bette Davis had expressed it onscreen in 1950, but by 1972, in the midst of the second-wave feminist revolution, retaining the same message in the play struck some reviewers as lazy and offensive to modern audiences. This, however, did nothing to diminish Lauren's appeal; her performance was lauded just as it had been in the States.

"If any musical needs a star, what *Applause* calls 'a biggie'—it's this one, and it's got one," wrote Helen Dawson of *The Observer*. "Lauren Bacall has a magnetism which even the hysteria of a first night audience couldn't discredit. The secret, I suppose, is style and sex—a vital, rangy sexuality which stamps itself all over the role."

The show played at Her Majesty's Theatre, a grand Victorian theater in Haymarket, and was sold out on most nights of its nearly year-long run. Before she was ready to let Margo Channing go for the final time, Lauren also agreed to appear in a filmed version of *Applause*, which would air as a TV special on CBS in 1973.

More theater work was to follow in the years to come. By now, Lauren considered herself more of a stage actress than a movie star —and yet, despite the enormous success of both *Cactus Flower* and *Applause*, despite the Tony Award and the glowing reviews, something was still missing. Few would disagree that she had the charisma and the star power to draw in audiences, but Bacall herself still felt insecure about her talent. There was still more to prove.

In 1977, she agreed to star in the national tour of the 1953 musical *Wonderful Town*. The show had plenty of personal connections for her: the music had been composed by her dear friend and Dakota neighbor, Leonard Bernstein, while the book was once again the work of her friends Betty Comden and Adolph Green. She starred as Ruth Sherwood, a role that had won Rosalind Russell a Tony back in 1953, and although many critics were generous about her efforts, the tour wasn't as successful as everyone had hoped. The problem, once again, was that the material appeared dated, and the production lacked the innovative vision which would have justified reviving a musical from a quarter-century before.

Then in 1980, she was approached about starring in another musical adaptation of a classic Hollywood movie—this time, she would be playing Tess Harding, the character made unforgettable by Katharine Hepburn in the 1942 Hepburn/Tracy comedy, *Woman of the Year*. She had some misgivings about accepting the role, chiefly the fact she'd once again play a part been created on film by another actress—and not just any actress. Just as Davis had been her heroine, Hepburn had not only been a close friend but also something of a personal idol. She knew that no matter how successful she'd be in the part, in the collective cultural memory, the role would always belong to Hepburn, just as

Margo Channing would always be indistinguishable from Bette Davis. But to have an entire production built as a star vehicle just for her, with Fred Ebb and John Kander writing the score, was impossible to decline.

It's curious that one more time she didn't have any sense that the plot of the film, even if superficially updated, would strike audiences as dated. The moral of the story was that a woman, no matter how successful and independent, is essentially only a real woman if she's standing by her man and creating a home for him. Such a message stood in striking contrast with the consensus of the second-wave feminist movement. Even if women such as Bacall, Hepburn, and Davis were often employed as icons of feminism, in truth, each of them had a complicated relationship with the women's liberation movement.

Tess Harding of the musical version was a morning TV anchor, reimagined in the vein of Barbara Walters. The script included numerous name-drops designed to convince the audience that the story was indeed contemporary. But the flaws still showed and many of the reviews picked up on them, particularly during the pre-opening tour.

"In updating *Woman of the Year*, (the creators) only dated it even more—so much so that it should probably be stamped: 'Perishable: Do not use after 1982,' as if it were a carton of milk," said one critic, summing up the consensus. Indeed, as of 2025, the show has never had a major revival.

Despite mixed reviews, the majority of critics were generous with Lauren, agreeing that she was the sole high point of the production. "The only reason that the show could, or would, run a long time in New York is Bacall," predicted the same reviewer. "Like Hepburn, she is a forceful original. She's gorgeous, she's stylish, she's bright, she's unique—in short, she's a genuine star." This prediction turned out to be correct: before *Woman of the Year* even opened on Broadway, it had secured four million dollars in advance ticket sales, an astronomical sum in 1981. No matter the reviews, the show was a hit.

"'I wrote the book on class,' sings Lauren Bacall in her new musical, and you better believe it," opened Frank Rich of the *New York Times* the day after *Woman of the Year* premiered at the Palace Theatre on

March 29, 1981. "This star's elegance is no charade, no mere matter of beautiful looks and gorgeous gowns. Her class begins where real class must—in her spirit." While Rich raved about her performance, he too thought the "gap between the star and her vehicle" to be "vast."

Regardless of its shortcomings, *Woman of the Year* scored six Tony nominations, winning four, including one for Bacall—her second win in the best actress in a musical category. The victory was a sweet vindication, an assurance of a permanent place among Broadway greats. The show would continue its successful run for a year. Lauren followed the familiar pattern of life while appearing in a play: rigorous and self-disciplined, with little socializing. She once again got involved with her leading man, the somewhat Bogart-esque Harry Guardino, but the relationship didn't survive beyond the duration of the run. Despite her loneliness, she avoided self-pity. "Listen, I'm a goddamned lucky lady. I know it," she told a journalist. "The best thing about getting older is that I don't care anymore what anyone thinks or says about me. I know who I am, where I've been, what I've done. And it ain't all bad, lemme tell you!"

Sadly, she would never again enjoy the same level of success on the New York stage. Nearly two decades would go by before she'd make a Broadway comeback in Noel Coward's comedy *Waiting in the Wings* in 1999. The show, in which she costarred with Rosemary Harris, would be a modest hit and a swansong to the stage career of Lauren Bacall.

CHAPTER 8

Lady in Distress

FOR LAUREN, THE 1970S WERE A TURBULENT TIME. ON THE ONE HAND, SHE reached great heights with the success of *Applause* and the subsequent Tony Award. She was now, at long last, a genuine Broadway star. On the other hand, movie offers had all but dried up, leaving her wondering if she would ever work in films again. She was also entering middle age, that dreaded time in the life of any actress, and she was facing it on her own. She felt restless, unsure about the future, and for the first time in her life, afraid of the passage of time. But retirement or self-pity were not an option. "When you're in the working mode, when all of you—your head, your senses—is pointed in that direction and there is no work for you, it is not only unsettling, it submerges you in almost total negativity," she later reflected on this period. "That is when you must invent new avenues for your talent—must expand your horizons if you are to prevail."

During a 1971 televised interview with Dick Cavett, Lauren was asked to single out two movies from her filmography she would save from a fire. Without hesitation she named *To Have and Have Not* as her first option before struggling to come up with a second choice. Torn between *The Big Sleep* and *Designing Woman*, she finally exclaimed: "I have not been in that many marvelous films, unfortunately!" This was perhaps a surprising statement from a woman who was already by this time considered a Hollywood legend.

"The problem with legends is that most of them are dead," she lamented. She would spend the better part of the 1970s trying to prove that she was far from dead, and that she still had a lot to offer. While the success of *Applause* helped to firmly establish her as a Broadway star, her film career stalled further, at one point seemingly reaching a point of no return. "When you're in a play, the movie world stops thinking of you," Lauren wrote years later. "They—the invisible 'they'—figure, Oh she's in a play, she doesn't want to make movies anymore, *if* they even think that."

As the women's movement was gaining traction, with winds of change gusting through the nation, Bacall entered the new decade on the cusp of this surging wave. Even if she was seen by many as an embodiment of the liberated female, she didn't possess enough clout in Hollywood to build a new career that would fit in with her independent spirit. Younger actresses, such as Jane Fonda and Faye Dunaway, were there to play the roles Lauren would have been so perfect for, had the change come, say a decade earlier. While sexism was rampant throughout the movie industry (and outside of it, too), ageism was yet another hurdle to overcome. Female actors who had come up during the studio era, particularly those whose public image relied heavily on glamour, found it virtually impossible to continue their screen careers past the age of forty. They also struggled to adapt to the new mode of production. After the collapse of the studio system, the industry, and the movies themselves, changed beyond recognition. But Lauren never saw herself as a screen goddess, and even if others perceived her as a glamorous movie star, she had always thought of herself as a character actress, able to play multiple roles, and she refused to step aside simply because the industry was ready to write her off. As Richard Brody noted in the *New Yorker*, "Bacall was bigger than her career. She started young and stayed ahead of her time."

Instead of a union leader or an investigative journalist, which would have suited her talents and the turbulent times, Lauren returned to the screen as Harriet Hubbard, a rich American widow, in the all-star adaptation of Agatha Christie's *Murder on the Orient Express*. Even if the film failed to provide her with the meaty material she craved for, it was nonetheless a flashy and glamorous supporting role, and Lauren injected it with a huge amount of wit and humor, elevating the character beyond the one-dimensional characterization it seemed to be on the page. The offer came unexpectedly, just as she was finishing her London run in *Applause*. Lauren loved London, and the prospect of extending her stay by a few months filled her with joy. Back home, Watergate was in full swing, and the political and social unrest that was tearing the country apart made her feel both grateful to be away, and guilty for somewhat dodging her civic responsibilities. On some level, boarding a 1930s train and playing make-believe murder mystery instead of taking active part in opposing Nixon and his administration felt to her like a betrayal.

Director Sidney Lumet assembled a truly impressive cast, with Albert Finney as Hercule Poirot, and featuring Ingrid Bergman, John Gielgud, Vanessa Redgrave, Michael York, Sean Connery, Anthony Perkins, Jacqueline Bisset, and Wendy Hiller. The film's producer, Richard Goodwin, remembers: "The cast were all such huge stars, yet somehow the film cost only $4.5 million. Were there any divas? No, they were all well behaved, although Lauren Bacall insisted on having her shoes made in Paris, Albert Finney got paid more because his Hercule Poirot had most of the lines, and Sean Connery got a percentage because he was such a big star. The rest all got paid the same, $100,000."

It was Lauren's first movie in eight years, and she would later call it "the happiest work experience" of her movie life. She found Lumet to be a supportive and extremely gifted director, and she formed a close bond with her costars. The cast would gather in the studio canteen to listen to John Gielgud's mesmerizing stories from his life in the theater, or to hear Vanessa Redgrave's political orations. Although none of their parts were particularly substantial, they were all happy to be involved. "They all did it for Sidney," Richard Goodwin reflects. "They loved him."

While she could have easily been lost in this sea of celebrated actors and famous names, Lauren radiated glamour and a certain confident energy, which she hadn't shown onscreen before. This was no doubt a result of her stage success; for the first time in her career she felt like she had something valuable to bring to the table, and that it was independent of anyone or anything else. Her character is key to the plot—she drives it as an instigator of the entire intrigue. Beside her luminous presence, Bacall delivers a strong, nuanced performance, and when viewing the film, one senses that Lumet has complete trust in her ability. Limited screen time doesn't prevent her from leaving a lasting impression on the viewer. Remembering the climactic scene, a flashback in which Harriet observes the twelve passengers plunge a dagger into a body, Lumet expressed his admiration for Lauren's work. He set up two cameras; one on the actors who came in to do the stabbing, and the second filming Bacall's reaction in close-up, all in one take. "I thought it would be of tremendous value to her building her character if we could do it in a single shot," Lumet later recalled. *Murder on the Orient Express* might just be the best example of Bacall's unique cinematic persona, that potent combination of movie star charisma with genuine ability to communicate emotional depth with just a single look. It isn't exactly craft in the way contemporary actors refer to it. Bacall wasn't a Method actor, nor did she have any defined technique to access those high emotional moments. What she does in scenes like her close-up reactions in *Murder* is purely instinctive, triggered by her complete confidence in the director. Her emotions are laid bare before the camera, the lens penetrating that famously sultry gaze to uncover something deeper, a truth born out of unguarded vulnerability. She wouldn't be able—or allowed to—access similar heights every time. In fact, she achieved it only a handful of times throughout her career. One is left to imagine how much potential was left unrealized and how many powerful performances were buried inside, for the lack of opportunity.

Reviews of her work on the film were positive, and the movie went on to become a commercial and critical success, earning six Oscar nominations, with Ingrid Bergman winning for best supporting actress. Although Finney and Bergman were the ones singled out for award-season glory, *Murder on the Orient Express* was truly an ensemble piece, and Lauren felt that all cast members deserved recognition. She no doubt felt a note of bitterness when Bergman picked up her third Oscar, tying her with Katharine Hepburn as the actor with most wins (Hepburn would eventually break this record in 1981 by winning for the fourth time for *On Golden Pond*). There's nothing to suggest that Bacall and Bergman were anything but cordial with each other during filming and the subsequent promotion of the film, despite the fact that Lauren never forgot the pain she had felt when Bergman snatched the role she had originated for the film version of *Cactus Flower*.

Even if Hollywood still wasn't ready to honor Lauren Bacall's work with as much as a single nomination for one of its prestigious trophies, it couldn't be denied that she continued to possess the skill and the star power to illuminate the screen as few others could. For Agatha Christie's part, although she was famously dismissive about adaptations of her work, she liked the film and would maintain that along with *Witness for the Prosecution*, Lumet's *Murder* was her favorite.

As soon as work on *Murder* wrapped, Lauren began planning her return to New York after a two-year absence. Leaving London was hard. She grew to love the city, its peaceful and dignified pace, and she cherished the friendships she made there. Sam, now thirteen, also felt settled in England, although he missed Jason. The years following his parents' divorce were particularly hard on Sam, who, as he later put it, grew up "basically alone." Robards was about to open in *A Moon for the Misbegotten* on Broadway, and Lauren felt that Sam ought to be near his father. And so, with boxes and crates filled with new memories they acquired during their time in London, Lauren and Sam returned to the Dakota in the spring of 1975. The shock of being back in the US hit them both, in different ways. For Lauren, the pressures of proving she was still relevant and could sustain her professional standing post-*Applause* soon resurfaced. She had no new job prospects, and the age-old actor's fear of never working again came upon her with a new force. New York seemed dirty and bleak, and Lauren could not shake the feeling that perhaps she would have been better off had she stayed in London.

Then came an unexpected offer to star alongside John Wayne in a movie adaptation of a Glendon Swarthout novel, *The Shootist*. It was to be filmed on location in Nevada, as well as on Warners' backlot in Hollywood, and although Lauren didn't find the part especially interesting, she accepted without much hesitation. For one thing, John Wayne personally asked for Lauren to be cast in the role, something she found incredibly moving and a little surprising. Even though they shared a warm and cordial working relationship on *Blood Alley* years earlier, Lauren had not realized that Wayne held her in such high regard. Their political views could hardly have been more opposing, but this seemed to be of little significance when it came to working together. Nearly two decades later Lauren would reflect: "I could totally disagree politically with someone like Duke, we would never move in the same circles, have the same interests, friends—yet I could really connect with him, care about him, even be attracted to him."

Wayne played a legendary assassin, the shootist of the title, who comes to stay at a small-town boarding house run by a middle-aged widow, Bond Rogers. She soon discovers that the man staying under her roof is not only the infamous gunfighter, but also that he is knocking on death's door, and that he has chosen her home as a place to die. The script was somber, and the scene in which Wayne's J. B. Books reveals to Bond that he is dying of cancer was no doubt difficult for both stars—for Lauren, flashbacks to Bogie's illness were inevitable (in fact, the last time she starred alongside Duke, Bogie *was* dying of cancer). For Wayne, the story hit home on an even more personal level: he had in fact been battling cancer since 1964. Although in remission at the time, the cancer would return and claim his life just three years later, making *The Shootist* his last screen appearance.

Throughout the shoot, especially while on location, Wayne's health was fragile, and Lauren, as well as the rest of the cast and crew, felt very protective of the legendary actor. It was clear to all that this could well be his last performance, a culmination of one of the most iconic acting careers in cinema's history. With little fast-paced, conventional Western action, the movie is essentially a character study, and as such it relies heavily on the emotional authenticity delivered by Wayne and Bacall in the scenes they share together. For her part, Lauren was brave enough to appear virtually makeup-free, without a hint of glamour, ready for the camera to showcase the mature beauty of her fifty-two-year-old face. She had never appeared more vulnerable or more powerful. Even if the scope of her role is limited, Bacall does some of her best work here, managing to build a character that is rich and multidimensional, and a perfect counterpart to Wayne's dying shootist.

When the film came out in August 1976, it was only moderately successful at the box office. Critics mostly disliked it. Rick Lenz, who played a supporting role in the film, reflected years later: "John Wayne was no longer the hot ticket in Hollywood at the time." Although for decades the Duke's films had consistently ranked among the top earners, by 1976 his Great American Hero persona seemed dated and out of step with the times. "If *The Shootist* develops any genuine nostalgia, it does so in spite of itself," wrote one critic. "When Bruce Surtees's camera picks up the craggy faces of Wayne, Bacall, and [James] Stewart, the scene itself no longer matters. Their faces tell the best story."

When it came to deliberating the aesthetics of onscreen aging, the press of the 1970s was relentless. It was especially true for female actors from the Golden Age; the tangible evidence of their mortality, of the fact that their faces succumbed to the same unforgiving reality the rest of the mere mortals dealt with, was something columnists and reviewers relished in. It made accepting any film role an act of bravery on the part of any of the women who wanted to continue working. Bacall was frustrated with the youth-obsessed culture of America.

"I'm so fed up with the preoccupation with youth," she said in an interview in 1985. "I'm so tired of everyone having face lifts and having to look good and have no lines, everyone competing with twenty-year-old girls—I mean, I think it is ridiculous. I may be cutting my own throat; it may be stupid—but I feel that you have to make yourself deal with things as they are. We all want to look better, everyone does, that's not original. But one gets older, younger people come up, that is the cycle of life. Nobody adores it, but that's the way it is."

For her performance in *The Shootist*, Lauren was nominated for the best actress BAFTA by the British Film Academy, yet another generous gesture by the country she came to love, and to which she was always happy to return.

Aside from a cameo role in Robert Altman's *HEALTH*, a bizarre satire in which she played an eighty-three-year-old virgin, Lauren would not appear onscreen again until 1981's *The Fan*. In the meantime, she kept herself busy working on her autobiography, a huge personal project that she began soon after returning from London. For years, she had toyed with the idea of writing, and yet she never felt ready to reveal herself on the page. But finally, as she later reflected, she needed a project that would distract her attention from the fact that work offers were not flooding in. She had found that once she started, the process of uncovering her own past brought her a sense of catharsis, and finally, closure. When *By Myself* came out in 1978, it became an instant bestseller, and the reviews were almost universally raves. In many ways, the book set a new standard for actors' autobiographies, primarily because Lauren was one of the first great stars of the Golden Age to pen her own story, without the help of a ghostwriter. She also did so mostly with candor and honesty, without sentimentality or self-glorification. Readers hoping to find any mention of Verita Thompson were in for a disappointment. As honest as she was, Bacall was not about to tarnish the legend of her relationship with Bogie. Much to her surprise, *By Myself* won the 1980 National Book Award for Autobiography. When the book was rereleased twenty-five years later, with an added chapter and retitled *By Myself . . . And Then Some*, some critics reviewed it unfavorably. Rachel Cooke of *The Guardian* concluded: "The chronology is there, but the insight is not." When viewed by today's standards of celebrity culture, the book perhaps falls short of delivering on the deep self-exploration front, although at the time of its release Bacall's candor was seen as a revelatory. *By Myself* remains a classic of the genre, and for Lauren it stood as one of her proudest achievements.

• • •

Still riding on the hype that surrounded the release of her book, Lauren began working on *The Fan* in the spring of 1980. The film told a story of an aging actress who is stalked by an obsessive and, as it turns out, lethally dangerous fan. With her autobiography remaining on the bestseller lists, the public's interest in her personal life was reinvigorated, and the film's producer, Robert Stigwood, whose previous credits included hugely successful musicals *Jesus Christ Superstar*, *Saturday Night Fever*, and *Grease*, was seeking to capitalize on Bacall's renewed popularity. Aside from Lauren, the cast consisted of the great Maureen Stapleton, James Garner, and a handsome newcomer, Michael Biehn, who was to play the deranged fan of the title. "I was very excited because it was Robert Stigwood, Lauren Bacall. It was huge," Biehn remembers. True to form, Stigwood did his best to spur media interest in the film even before the cameras started rolling. Biehn, who had previously worked in television, recalls "flying into New York, and all that Stigwood press bonanza. I was more intimidated about being in such a big production than I was about working with Lauren Bacall." In the end, Biehn made Douglas Breen a memorably creepy and complex character. Although today Biehn doesn't consider *The Fan* a particularly important entry in his filmography, the movie did pave the way for him to subsequently have a successful, if brief, movie career, with credits including *The Terminator* and *Aliens*.

Even if Biehn had the flashy, titular role, there was no doubt that Lauren Bacall was the true star of the movie. *The Fan* was perhaps the closest she ever got to a star vehicle—for the first, and only time in her career, she was *the* star of a film. She wasn't there to support a leading man, to serve as a tough counterpart to an even tougher male actor—this time it was her show, and Lauren was going to enjoy it.

The part of Sally Ross mirrored her own life to such a degree that at times it seemed as though the lines between reality and fiction were, at the very least, blurred. Ross, like Bacall, is a larger-than-life star, with a luminous Hollywood past, who has reinvented herself as a star of the Broadway stage. She lives alone in a plush New York apartment building, which, not unlike the Dakota, overlooks Central Park. Her flat is filled with mementos of her illustrious career and pictures of her famous friends. Naturally, the production designers didn't need to work very hard to find such photos of Lauren. Featured in the movie are iconic images of Bacall sitting on the piano (which is being played by Harry Truman), as well as photos of her with Olivier and Vivien Leigh, and with Ingrid Bergman.

What made the film enjoyable for Lauren was the fact that she was able to work in New York, returning to her own apartment at the end of each day—a luxury rarely afforded to actors while working on a movie. Many of her scenes featured Maureen Stapleton, a seasoned veteran of the stage, who the following year would win an Oscar for her performance in *Reds*. Lauren found her a dream to work with; she knew she had to stretch all her acting muscles to prevent Stapleton from stealing all the scenes from her. The two worked well together and their onscreen chemistry is a delight to watch. Less cordial was her relationship with Michael Biehn. The young actor found Lauren to be rude and difficult, even if their scenes together amounted to little over two days of shooting. He was also unimpressed with her legendary status: "I thought that she was just good casting. There was nothing in her work, previous to this, that made me think 'Oh, I'm really gonna have to put my acting shoes on.'" For her part, Lauren resented shooting the final scenes of the movie, the only ones she shared with Biehn, which could account for her less-than-generous behavior. The final confrontation between Sally and her obsessive fan required a great deal of physical roughness, and Lauren objected to it, to no avail.

As far as she was concerned, *The Fan* was a psychological piece, exploring the lonely and at times dangerous life of an actress. Later, she expressed disappointment that director Edward Bianchi chose to refocus the story, emphasizing the slasher horror aspect of it. In fact, it was Stigwood's idea to turn the film bloody. After the financial success of *Dressed to Kill* and *Friday the 13th*, both of which came out while the production on *The Fan* was underway, Stigwood ordered the script to be rewritten to fit with what he saw as a new and profitable trend. Bianchi remembers having to go back and reshoot certain scenes, on

Stigwood's request. "It was the slasher elements that Lauren wasn't happy about," Bianchi later recalled. "We were both fighting all the time to try and keep it as a psychological thriller, and we were getting undermined all the time."

"The movie I wanted to make had more to do with what happens to the woman—and less blood and gore," Lauren later told an interviewer. "*The Fan* is much more graphic and violent than when I read the script."

Whatever her misgivings about the final version, Lauren emerged from it unscathed. Unlike many horror movies featuring mature actresses, *The Fan* doesn't exploit or victimize Bacall. Rather than appearing as a grotesque caricature of an aging actress, she portrays a woman in charge of her own destiny and a successful professional. Even if the film's exploration of aging and loneliness can be viewed as stereotypical and at times ultra-camp, there are moments of rare insight, especially scenes in which Lauren is alone in her apartment and, later, at her Hamptons beach house. But perhaps most importantly, the film allows its heroine to be her own savior. While throughout the movie Sally seeks protection in the arms of her ex-husband (James Garner) and Inspector Andrews (Hector Elizondo), in the end she must confront Breen herself—and she emerges victorious in the process. Few female characters are ever given so much agency, particularly in the horror movie genre, and in that sense *The Fan* remains a rare gem. Despite containing a highly disturbing and somewhat exploitative scene in which Douglas Breen seduces and murders a young gay man, after which he proceeds to burn his body, the film remains a cult classic, not least with gay audiences. This is no doubt due to its camp aesthetics, the idealization of Bacall's larger-than-life star persona, and the musical numbers, including Lauren's smoky-voiced rendition of "Hearts not Diamonds." To this day, Michael Biehn is still surprised by how often he is approached by gay fans expressing their love for the movie.

When the filming on the picture wrapped in the summer of 1980, no one could have predicted that within months, the film's narrative would prove tragically prophetic. On December 8, John Lennon, who had been Lauren's neighbor at the Dakota for the past seven years, was shot and killed outside the apartment building. His assassin, Mark David Chapman, was an obsessive fan, eerily resembling Douglas Breen. Lauren was profoundly shocked at the news. With the attention of the world's media suddenly directed, quite literally, at her front door, she was also upset that her place of residence was now public knowledge. "The ghouls are outside nonstop with their goddamn cameras," she complained. Despite having recently written an autobiography, she remained one of the most guarded and private of celebrities; she simply didn't believe that she owed the public, and especially the media, anything beyond her work and what she chose to share.

The morbid hype that surrounded *The Fan*, even before its release, eventually went on to work against the film's favor when it came out the following May. The studio chose to open the movie with an exclaimer denying similarities between the film and Lennon's death. Lauren found this to be a cheap and tasteless way to get attention. "I think it's disgusting, revolting and exploitative," she told *People*. "Obviously, whoever decided to do it thought that it would help the movie. I think it will hurt it."

In the end, for all the publicity, *The Fan* failed to attract a large audience, and it was a commercial disappointment. It was also largely panned by critics. Lauren, however, received mostly good reviews, with most critics agreeing that she was the highlight of the film. "*The Fan* has several terrific things going for it, and they're all named Lauren Bacall," wrote Vincent Canby in the *New York Times*. He went on to state: "Miss Bacall transforms an essentially creaky, lady-in-distress thriller into something approaching a cinematic event." Lauren was delighted with the good notices. "I'm thrilled. I've never had such a good review for a film," she confessed to a journalist. "I think I'll run away with Vincent Canby," she added with laughter.

CHAPTER 9

At Home

LAUREN LIVED AT THE DAKOTA FOR MORE THAN HALF A CENTURY. SHE HAD first moved in back in 1960, at the start of her relationship with Jason. At first, she leased her spacious three-bedroom apartment, but soon, benefiting from Dakota's recent transformation into a co-op, she was able to buy it—one of the first tenants to do so. It was to be one of the best investments she had ever made—not just in terms of its real-estate value, which would over the decades increase exponentially, but also as an emotional investment. The fourth-floor apartment, number 43, with its towering high ceilings, picture windows, half of which overlooked Central Park, and original Victorian details, would remain a refuge, a place where she would store all her treasures, where she'd see her children grow, a nest from which all three would flee, a sanctuary where she'd rest, receive friends, and eventually, the place where she'd leave this life.

Gradually, as the years went by, she shaped it, made each room a unique creation of her taste, a result of the people she'd known, the places she'd visited, the life she'd lived. There was the library—a room overflowing with rare books, some inscribed to her by author friends—this was her favorite cozy spot to sit and read, go over her lines, rehearse her musical numbers, spend time with close friends. A formal drawing room, with a piano where her friend and neighbor,

Leonard Bernstein, would sit and play for her. The dining room where she'd host dinner parties—theater friends, politicians, her family. Thanksgivings and Christmases. The third bedroom would in time become a study. Her own master suite was a boudoir fit for a movie queen. The walls of the entire apartment were covered with rare and important works of art. David Hockney. Jim Dine. Chagall. There were also works by friends like Ted Kennedy, Henry Fonda, and Noel Coward.

The sculptures of Henry Moore were among her most prized possessions. She had loved his work since the 1950s, when she was introduced to it by her friend, the wife of Bogie's agent, Mildred Jaffe, and had purchased some of his lithographs. She'd subsequently amassed an impressive number of his bronze sculptures, including "Maquette for Mother and Child: Arms" and "Working Model for Reclining Figure: Bone Skirt." In 1976, she traveled to the artist's English country house to meet him—of all the illustrious figures she had encountered over the years, Moore was the one she had been most star-struck by.

"There is no way possible to articulate my feeling after my visit to Much Hadham [Moore's town]," Lauren wrote in a letter to the artist. "Since then, and my return to New York, I have thought and thought of that day. It was and will ever be a high point in my life, the realization of a dream—to actually meet you and spend time with you. Some say it is dangerous to meet one's idols, but in your case—and this is true—you were far beyond expectation."

Robert Graham's bronze statues of nude female forms were also among her favorites. Graham, married to Lauren's close friend, Anjelica Huston, was someone she was fascinated by. Whenever she was on the West Coast, she'd pay a visit to the house Graham and Huston shared in Venice Beach, often returning to New York with yet another one of Robert's bronze sculptures—one particular figure, named Gabrielle, bore the personalized inscription, "For Betty," another, called Christine, "For Lauren." Graham's pencil drawings of nudes also adorned her hall walls; many were dedicated to her.

And of course, there were the photos. Portraits of her friends and colleagues, those who influenced her, touched her heart. A large drawing of Spencer Tracy sat on top of the piano. Candid shots of Vivien Leigh, and of Larry Olivier and Joan Plowright, Olivier's third wife, whom Lauren got to know and like, despite her enduring loyalty to Vivien. Other dear friends, like Mildred Jaffe, Slim Hawks, Roddy McDowall, Gregory Peck, and John Huston. The self-portrait Katie Hepburn had given her on the occasion of Lauren winning her first Tony. Some portraits of herself, like the gorgeous drawing done by Jean Negulesco, which had once graced the cover of the French edition of *Vogue* and a striking profile by Aaron Shikler. Although Bacall was a social snob, the photos were not a mere "look-who-I've-met" kind of a display—all the faces looking silently on from them were of people who had played a big part in her life. She'd not only rubbed shoulders with some of the most iconic figures of the twentieth century, but she had lived alongside them, was their friend, was one herself.

She had never sought the help of a decorator. Her apartment was her own, a tapestry of stories, some of which would remain untold. Each object, each picture, representing a moment in time, a special encounter, a beloved person, a moment of professional triumph. Some entering her fabled home were overwhelmed at the sheer number of objects.

"As anyone can see upon entering my apartment, I am a collector of many things," she explained in 1978. "For many years, pewter, plates, mugs, you name it—brass, snuffboxes, match strikers, faience animals, needlepoint, ivory animals, bronze animals, boxes—all are antiques. All have lived through a lot. All make me feel warm. The place *is* cluttered—but it is personal. And in each room, as you wander down the hall, there is something else. There are a lot of books too, with one on Henry Moore in each room. Also pictures of my friends. My friends, and my children. All important to me. And my dog. I'm attached to it all."

Surprisingly to some, there wasn't a great deal of Bogie in the apartment. No photos from their iconic films, nothing ostentatious. And yet, for those who looked closely and knew Bacall well, there were signs of him scattered throughout. Pieces of jewelry he had given her. The striking Segovia paintings they'd bought together in Paris. Books they had found in dusty bookstores and read together. And then, there was the bronze statuette of Bogie as Sam Spade, made by Guss Strehle, which stood on one of the side tables.

She loved the Dakota. She could enjoy her privacy there—a place right in the heart of Manhattan, and yet, somewhat removed, a world all to itself. The sheer vastness of the apartment—4,000 square feet—and the building's unique old-world architecture meant that Lauren didn't have to worry about noisy neighbors, babies crying behind thin walls, loud parties. The Dakota was filled with interesting characters, many famous and celebrated names, from Lenny Bernstein to Roberta Flack, and since 1971, John Lennon and Yoko Ono. Lennon's murder on December 8, 1980, shook Lauren, just as it had everyone else, but to the famous residents of the Dakota, the fear evoked by the tragedy was tangible. Lauren was at the time in the middle of rehearsing for *Woman of the Year*, a show she'd be performing live in front of thousands of strangers, eight times a week. Having just completed filming *The Fan*, the plot of which had so closely and eerily predicted real events, she was justifiably terrified, although, true to her character, she hated to admit it. When the film critic and her Dakota neighbor Rex Reed named her as one of the building's residents during a live TV interview, she flew into a rage. It mattered little that she had been famously associated with the Dakota before then; she saw the fact that Reed would use her name during such a tense and sensitive time as an abuse, another proof that the press couldn't be trusted. Reed later complained that Bacall called him up, screaming down the phone. She refused to apologize.

"What bugs me, what has always bugged me, what always bugged Bogie, is the God-dammed press and its assumption that actors are not private human beings," she later explained, still angered. "I think the press was really irresponsible printing those photos of Steve McQueen dead. And the John Lennon thing! I was there when Lennon was shot and I can't believe what they did on television, a sideshow, a disgrace! Sure, I know what Rex Reed did, all that ghoulish stuff, just because he lives at the Dakota too, and speaking out as though he represented all of us in the building. Lenny [Bernstein] was ready to kill him. You bet your ass I called Rex Reed and screamed at him."

Some saw Lauren's outbursts as insensitive to Lennon's memory and the situation, making it about her privacy rather than the man who had just lost his life. Reed would have his own revenge on Bacall a few months later, penning a vicious, damaging review of *Woman of the Year* after it opened that March. In the piece, entitled "How Long Can Bacall Hold Up a Disaster?," Reed writes: "The question remains, how long can Lauren Bacall sell tickets with nothing going for her but charisma?" Reed's poisonous pen no doubt hurt Lauren, especially that other reviews of the show weren't strong. But no other critic aimed so directly at her, and Reed's vindictiveness was obvious. He did, however, touch upon some raw nerves, questioning areas that had been sources of insecurity for her for many years. She was not a trained dancer or singer—neither was she known for her dramatic range—and the success of her musicals relied heavily on her star power. But who was Reed to criticize her? What gave any of the critics the right to dismiss months and months of hard work with a single, ill-thought review? The episode with Reed left her bitter and resentful, so much so that during an appearance on the Johnny Carson show, two years later, she complained: "It is my feeling that in most cases, they [the critics] have been unsuccessful as either playwrights, or novelists, or any other kind of writer, or performers, or some other field. What is left for them is to sit and knock everybody else." There could be little doubt that she was specifically referencing Reed, who had indeed been a failed actor. In later years, the two would patch things up, even becoming unlikely friends—or at least, frenemies. After Lauren's death, Reed once again took to his typewriter, paying her a tribute, which, unsurprisingly, he one last time studded with sour notes. "To Bogie she was Baby, to her friends she was Betty, and I was lucky enough to be counted as one of them," he wrote. "No longer sultry and glamorous like the siren who lit up 1940s film noirs, she could be thorny and difficult, acting like a self-centered dowager when her limo blocked the entrance to the basement of the Dakota apartments in the dark days following the murder of John Lennon." Reed went on to recall that things between them changed after a driver, who'd come to pick them up for a charity event Lauren agreed to appear at with Reed, referred to her as "Mrs. Reed." "I held my breath, fearing the beginning of World War III, but she laughed all night." After that, whenever Lauren was bedridden, Reed would offer to walk her dog. She'd always sign her thank-you notes to him as "Mrs. Reed."

Lauren's Dakota residence had over the years become part of her legend. It was *hers* alone—it symbolized her life after Bogie, her independence, a building block of her mythology. She was one of the Golden Age goddesses who had chosen to make Manhattan their home. There was, of course, Garbo, whose plush apartment on East Fifty-second Street became her hideaway from the world. Katharine Hepburn lived in a beautiful Turtle Bay brownstone townhouse, the same she had bought all the way back in 1931. Joan Crawford lived out her days in the Upper East Side's Imperial House, across the park from the Dakota. They were the rarest of those rare urban jungle cats, mythical creatures, to be glanced at occasionally exiting a taxi, dining at Elaine's or Sardi's, shopping on Fifth Avenue. Although Bacall hated to be thought of as a legend, by the 1980s, she had unequivocally become one.

Her legend wasn't entirely made up of flattering myths and anecdotes. Over the years, plenty of people have spoken out about Bacall's less-than-kind side. She could be bitchy, entitled, and difficult. She was often demanding, impatient, moody. She hated hypocrisy, detested small talk, had no time for ignorance or unprofessionalism. Some, like her long-time hairstylist Judy Crown, thought her downright mean. Others, like author Michael Michaud, whose first job after moving to Los Angeles in the 1970s was working at the Magic Nut and Fruit Company at the Farmers' Market, remember Bacall as "not overtly friendly but not rude at all."

"Not long after I started working there, Lauren Bacall approached the stall," remembers Michaud. "She must have been on the West Coast for a movie. I saw her coming and noticed that the other folks I worked with all seemed to scatter, look away, or preoccupy themselves. They later told me she was a frequent customer and was very difficult to accommodate. She stepped up to the glass counter, looked directly at me, and said, 'What nice person is going to wait on me today?' I was the last man standing.

"She requested a specially packed box of various flavored candy corn to send to her son, Sam Robards, who was attending a private school on the East Coast. The shop had several combinations to choose from, and we were instructed to sell those, but she didn't like any of them, and wanted to pick and choose what she wanted from our stock. I was new on the job, and didn't know what the rules were, so I just pulled together whatever she wanted for the delivery. She knew what she wanted, and I suspect had no time for anyone who might disagree with her.

"The shop provided complementary gift cards to customers to enclose with their package. I gave her one. She wrote a note to her son and handed it back to me. I handed her a gift card and asked her to autograph it for me. She sort of smiled, signed it, and thanked me. She asked my name, and said, 'I'm going to ask for you next time, Michael.' And she did. I later peeked. She wrote, 'Miss you, love Mom,' on the card for her son. I waited on her several other times. She was never rude to me, and, of course, I packaged whatever she asked for. I liked waiting on her and felt a little special. I waited on many celebrities while I worked there—she was one of my favorites."

She was noted for her intelligence and wry sense of humor, which she was always quick to apply to any situation, not least of all, to herself. In the summer of 1987, writer Nat Segaloff, who at the time worked as a reporter for the *Boston Globe*, was given exclusive access to the filming location of Danny Huston's film, *Mr. North*. Lauren was among those in the cast, and Segaloff recalls that she could be "a handful" at times, but he quickly adds: "I adored her."

"Her best kept secrets are her fragility, her sweetness, and her softness," reflects Anjelica Huston, who grew up with her father's stories of Bacall, and who'd in subsequent years become a close friend. "To know her is to see all of that, to see how vulnerable she is. And that's what makes her such a great actress too."

Frederic Goldrich, who worked with Bacall in the summer tour of *Wonderful Town* in 1977, remembered her with fondness. "She could certainly be blunt, she didn't mince words, but she was never mean or unkind," Goldrich recalled. "When I met her, she was in her fifties, and although singing and dancing weren't her strongest points, she worked extremely hard and was always friendly with everyone in the company. She was still a great beauty and commanded respect—but she was also a lot of fun, joking about herself, talking freely with everyone. I wasn't aware of anyone in the company disliking her."

When Merv Griffin interviewed her in 1987, Bacall spoke frankly about her reputation as a "tough broad": "I don't pay any attention to labels. The only thing I don't like about the pigeonhole section of my life is when I've been called 'tough.' Because I don't feel that strength means tough. I don't agree with the notion that strong women are bitches. I mean, I know I'm not a bitch. I know that Katie Hepburn is not a bitch. I know that in life, particularly if you're a woman alone, you develop a kind of veneer that protects you."

• • •

New York and the Dakota might have been her home, but there were other places, other cities she loved and felt she also belonged to. For about a decade, starting in the mid-1970s, she owned a charming country house in Amagansett, East Hampton. She loved the countryside, walks by the beach, her garden. In the end, the physical and financial strain of maintaining a house became too overwhelming, and she reluctantly agreed to sell it. Ever since she had visited Paris and London for the first time in the early 1950s, she felt a strong connection to both. London meant warm friendships, a break from the fast-paced life in the States. It also usually signaled a fulfilling professional venture. In the fall of 1984, she was asked to star in the London revival of Tennessee Williams's *Sweet Bird of Youth*, to be directed by the great Harold Pinter. It was the kind of offer she had long waited for—a rich, complex part in a straight play by one of the greats. The role of Alexandra "the Princess" del Lago, an aging, larger-than-life movie queen, had been originally portrayed by Geraldine Page, who also reprised her performance in the 1963 movie version, starring opposite Paul Newman and earning an Oscar nomination. Page wouldn't be an easy act to follow; considered one of the most gifted actresses of her generation, she had left a stamp on the work, just as had Bette Davis on *All About Eve* and Katharine Hepburn on *Woman of the Year*. But Bacall was in many ways better equipped to play del Lago. She had known firsthand the heights of movie stardom, the veneration of being seen as a sultry beauty, and the perils of trying to hold on to success in an unforgiving, youth-obsessed industry. She had experienced relationships with younger men, and the insecurities that accompanied them. She was a professional woman, living alone, facing the same anxieties Williams's heroine did.

"When I started to play her, I was living alone in London, with my three children in America," she later wrote. "I could relate to the Princess. I was less manic, less extreme, but as I went along night after night, the weeks growing to months, I made many discoveries. With a writer like Tennessee Williams, there are always endless layers to his characters.

"His kind of writing does almost all the work, and Tennessee was one of the few playwrights in my lifetime who could provide it. He made me feel that I was a better actress. I could be reckless, could let go, I could rise to the occasion. And if not—I could come close. Closer than I ever had before."

English actor Andrew Roberts, who was at time fresh out of drama school, was thrilled to land his first job as an understudy and a walk-on in Harold Pinter's production. He later remembered working with Lauren: "It was Lauren Bacall, already a legend and the star of the production. And I got to call her Betty. This shouldn't happen to a kid from Wolverhampton like me, but there she was, still beautiful at sixty—and that voice! Every night of the run, I would stand in the wings and watch the first scene. She walked downstage center, lifted her head, threw back her hair, and as the light hit that extraordinary face the audience gasped. Every night. There was the legend, right there in front of them." Roberts also recalls that outside of the show, as imperious as her presence was, Bacall acted simply as one of the gang. "Bacall was a movie star, but she was also an actor just like the rest of us. As a company, we went out to Joe Allen restaurant, Bacall table-hopping with her glass of Stoli, talking to all of us. We were all equals."

Working with Pinter was a thrilling experience for her. As a writer, he understood the importance of words, particularly when written by a poetic genius like Williams. Lauren trusted Pinter, and the two developed a close friendship that endured for years thereafter. "Oh, Harold is one of my heroes!" she later recalled. "Plus, opening in London was amazing because it's one of my favorite places in the world. It's the greatest theater city in the world."

The love was mutual, as most of her reviews were highly complimentary after the show opened at the Haymarket Theatre Royal. "To watch this lady in action is to appreciate how a legend was built," noted one review. "Here is an actress not living on past celluloid memories. . . . Rather adapting to the stage by being unafraid of playing 'big,' and by bringing to it the great quality of presence. She is quite magnificent."

Ros Asquith of *The Observer* called her "slinky as a lynx, hot as pepper, cool as rain, dry as smoke," before adding that "there's considerably more to her than staying sexy at sixty."

His colleague at *The Observer,* Melvyn Bragg, met Bacall backstage at the Theatre Royal Plymouth during an out-of-town tour, before the London opening. "I've never seen bone structure like it, and the face, the skin, all that," he notes in his article. "All natural, no scissor-and-paste job anywhere. Sensational. That's the answer: that's how she looks."

Sweet Bird of Youth ran successfully in London for over six months, after which Lauren agreed to take the show to Australia. She had never worked there before and was excited at the prospect; the cast would change almost entirely, and she'd need to adjust her performance accordingly. Although her reviews were excellent, the relationship with the Aussie press was to be a troubled one. Things hit stormy waters soon after her arrival, with a front-page article and interview in the *Sydney Morning Herald*. "Bacall Better than Bogie?" asked the headline provocatively. The interviewer for the paper, Evan Whitton, in a rare display of tactlessness, launched into Lauren from the get-go, but true to form, she didn't let him get away with anything without putting up a good fight.

"Well, how are you playing *Sweet Bird*?" opened Whitton.

"HOW? The best that I can. I don't know what you mean by how . . ."

The interview only got more awkward until Whitton, with no apparent logic behind his statement, fired:

"Can I say this? On any analysis, you are more talented than your late husband."

"I am WHAT?" she asked, thrown. "I don't understand why you would say that. . . . I don't consider myself more talented than Bogie at all, not by any stretch of the imagination. Different talents, he didn't live very long so. . . ."

She was clearly upset and regretted agreeing to do the interview. It was too late. The piece, along with an especially unflattering picture of her, was Australia's welcome gift. Things wouldn't improve—press items continued to appear, some falsely claiming that the show was a box-office bomb, others reporting on Lauren's supposed statements about Australia.

"I just disembarked to get into a car, and suddenly all this garbage was printed in the newspapers about me—all made up. All I did was walk off an airplane," she complained during a press conference in Brisbane. A female journalist followed up with: "Miss Bacall, after your comments, I'm sure you must agree with Frank Sinatra who described Australian journalists as hookers. Is that how you feel about the media in Australia?"

"Now, would you say that that was a fair question?" Bacall retorted slowly. "I don't know what Frank said when he was here, I know he had problems when he was here, and I'm not surprised." Despite all the unpleasantness, the Australian tour was a success, and Lauren would later write: "I think I was better in Australia. I hope I was, I should have been."

• • •

"I don't understand people who retire, I've never been able to figure that out, it doesn't make any sense to me," Lauren said in 1995. "I still want to prove something I suppose. I still want to show that I can do it, and that I can do more than people think I can. I want to use myself—I look forward to work."

Work continued to be a driving force for her. If film roles didn't materialize—and good scripts were now few and far between—she did television movies, hosted documentaries or appeared in her now-iconic High Point Coffee commercials. Anything to keep herself busy. In 1978, she agreed to appear in her first full-length TV movie, the Nora Ephron-scripted *Perfect Gentlemen*. The film was a crime comedy, with a stellar cast of female talents, including Sandy Dennis and Ruth Gordon. Lauren plays a wealthy and elegant wife of an embezzled crook, who, during her weekly jail visits with her husband, forms an unlikely friendship with two of the other visiting wives. The movie boasts Ephron's signature hilarious dialogue, and it's a joy to watch Bacall and Sandy Dennis perfectly complement each other's comedic styles—Bacall's dry and witty, Dennis's erratic and unpredictable.

A decade later, she was back on TV for the remake of George Cukor's 1933 pre-Code classic *Dinner at Eight*. Lauren played a famous writer, updated for the 1980s, a self-described "official talk show dowager slut." She was generally pleased with her performance, although she complained that the number of ads on TNT ruined anyone's chances of actually enjoying the movie. Reviewers pointed out that Bacall was much better suited for the part than Marie Dressler had been in the original.

"Playing it broadly (in every sense of the word), Dressler was a far cry from the glamorous Carlotta Vance she was supposed to be," wrote Harry Haun in the *Daily News*. "Bacall, on the other hand, is Bacall—middle name Glamor—and she gives the role the full twinkle n' shine."

It was that twinkle n' shine, the glamour and star quality she exuded, that producers now wanted her for. It bothered her—she still wanted to be challenged, to be seen as a character actress, rather than simply lending her legendary name to projects which offered her little in return. She entered the 1990s with a small role in Rob Reiner's adaptation of Stephen King's *Misery*. The part of James Caan's literary agent could have easily been played by any other actor, but Reiner wanted someone with a touch of class, and he certainly came to the right place. Bacall injects wit and style into her character, taking full advantage of every frame of film she appears in, although Reiner doesn't give her much to do. *Misery* became a sleeper hit, both with critics and audiences, culminating in the Oscar for best actress for Kathy Bates. Once again, Lauren Bacall was both current and legendary—she had entered the sixth decade of her professional career riding high. She might not have been the star of the film, but she was still working and was in demand. There were few other "big names" from the Golden Age who were able to sustain the same level of activity, and few had Bacall's determination to do so.

A year after *Misery*, she teamed up with Anthony Quinn for a French-Canadian coproduction, *A Star for Two*. Upon its release, the independent film was seen by few, but it did give Lauren the chance to act opposite Quinn, and in a rare leading role. "I don't get many brilliant roles," she admitted soon after she finished shooting. "Women have not had an easy time. I hope that will change in some areas. I think now that the filmmakers realize *Rambo* and *Rocky* are not working. Relationships between older people are far more interesting, and I believe the public wants to see that."

She got another shot at exploring the theme of mature relationships in 1993, when she appeared in the TV movie *The Portrait*, again for TNT. The film reunited Lauren with her dear friend Gregory Peck, with whom she hadn't worked since *Designing Woman*. It was a strange, touching experience—how different things were now. The last time they acted together, Bogie was still alive. Peck's grownup daughter, Cecilia, who hadn't even been born at the time of *Designing Woman*, played their onscreen daughter.

The Portrait is a tender character piece, with Peck and Lauren conveying the true intimacy of a couple who had been sharing life for decades. Peck, who was coproducing the movie, suggested Lauren for the role, while his daughter sought to hire Arthur Penn as a director—both agreed. "I've known Betty longer than almost anybody," Peck said at the time. "We've kept up our friendship over the years. We appeared to be a real family on the screen."

It was a lovely reunion, but it was in no way a swansong to Lauren's acting career, as some papers predicted. Now entering her seventies, Lauren Bacall was far from done.

CHAPTER 10

Curtain Call

IN THE SPRING OF 1994, LAUREN TRAVELED TO PARIS—ONE OF HER FAVORITE cities—to appear in Robert Altman's all-star production *Pret-a-Porter* (later titled *Ready to Wear* in the US). The part of a fashion editor, Slim Chrysler (a tribute to Slim Hawks as well as to Lauren's *To Have and Have Not* character) wasn't a great one—she was once again offering her legendary status to a project which required little of her, but she adored Altman and could not turn down the opportunity to live and work in Paris. She set up in an elegant apartment on the Left Bank and whenever not needed on set, immersed herself in Parisian life—museums, cafés, old friends. The film's cast was indeed impressive, ranging from European film royalty, Marcello Mastroianni and Sophia Loren to Hollywood's current It Girl, Julia Roberts. Altman gathered one of the most glittering ensembles ever featured in a single movie. Sadly, the sheer amount of talent in front of the camera wasn't enough to save the film, which upon its release over the 1994 Christmas season was a critical and financial bomb. Being part of the film, however, once again proved that Bacall was still in vogue, still very much a working actor, not just a relic of the past. "She never got locked in any time wrap," Altman reflected in an interview. "Think about how many social and attitudinal changes that have occurred, and yet Bacall has always remained unique."

In May of 1995, she got a call from Barbra Streisand, who was casting her latest movie, *The Mirror Has Two Faces*. She wanted to meet with Lauren to talk about the part of her cinematic mother. Streisand had originally envisaged Gena Rowlands in the role, but scheduling conflicts prevented Rowlands from accepting the offer. As ever, Lauren felt crippling nerves as she headed for Streisand's New York apartment. Even after five decades in the business, she was still auditioning, still expected to prove she was good enough. The character of Hannah Morgan was the best part she had been offered in years. While certainly a supporting role, she had many shades and dimensions, allowing the actress who'd portray her to dive deep and showcase a wide range of skills, from comic timing to pathos.

In her memoir, Bacall recalls being shown around the apartment by Streisand before an informal reading—a nonaudition that felt very much like an audition. "As I headed for the door, Barbra said, 'So, you could play my mother?'" Lauren writes. "'Yes, I can play your mother,' I replied. 'Though, come to think of it, I would have had to be a teenage mother to qualify.'" There was a mere seventeen years between the two, but it mattered not—in the world of Hollywood movies, gaps between parents and children have been known to be in the single digits.

For about a week, she was on tenterhooks, anxiously awaiting news from her agent, before finally being told that the part was hers. The shoot would take place in New York, giving Lauren the rare opportunity to live at home while working. Streisand's reputation as a perfectionist and a control freak had been the stuff of Hollywood lore for years, but Lauren knew all too well that showbiz gossip was often exaggerated, particularly when it came to women. She had known Barbra since the 1960s; she saw her performing on the opening night of *Funny Girl* on Broadway, instantly captivating Lauren along with everyone else who saw it.

From the start of filming, Streisand was impressed with Lauren's dedication to the character and to the project. Bacall had always understood that film was a director's medium, and she had always respected that, letting herself be transformed into whatever vision was required of her. This was certainly the right approach to adopt with Streisand, who had very definitive ideas about each and every element of the movie—from costumes and set decorations to the film's soundtrack, and, of course, the actors' interpretations. She nonetheless welcomed creative input and was happy when Bacall made a suggestion to make Hannah a working woman. "Lauren had a very good idea, because the mother didn't work in the first script," Streisand later recalled. "And she said, 'Well, what does she do all day? Because you have to cook dinner for her.' And I said, 'You know, that is a good idea, you should go to work.'" Inspired by the mother of a childhood friend, Streisand decided to make Hannah a beautician, which fits well with the movie's theme of beauty and its many faces.

Filming progressed through the winter months of 1995 and into 1996. It happened to be one of the toughest New York winters on record, with blizzards and cold weather often halting production and causing delays. Most of Lauren's scenes were filmed inside a replica of the Upper West Side apartment, which for the sake of the film had been recreated on a soundstage at Harlem's 142nd Street Armory. The pairing of Streisand and Bacall was a hot topic for gossip columnists who predicted a clash between the two Hollywood divas. "They ought to get along like a 50-room house afire," wrote Liz Smith in her column. "These two are very strong women—big stars. But under their tough and controlling images, they are basically insecure, vulnerable to the max, and yes—even lovable." For the most part, they worked well together. Streisand noted that Lauren was often nervous and tended to overact in her scenes. In order to get the best out of her, Barbra would instruct her cameraman to continue shooting, even after she called "cut." Some of Bacall's best moments in the film are therefore at least partially improvised. This included the scene in which Rose (Streisand's character) asks her mother what it had been like to be beautiful. It wasn't easy for Lauren to think of herself as a beauty icon, even if she had been seen as one since her movie debut. "I always saw what was wrong," she once confessed to an interviewer. "I saw the crooked teeth, the imperfections. And that was what I paid attention to as opposed to the positives. That's maybe one of my hangups and problems. I certainly never thought I was a raving beauty, and I was not. I've seen raving beauties; I know what raving beauties look like." Lauren's initial reaction to Rose's question was to exclaim, "Wonderful, wonderful!" Streisand knew she could get something more authentic from her. As the camera was being reset, she took Lauren aside. "You know, Betty, when you did all those movies with Humphrey Bogart and all that, what was that like?" Lauren paused and thought back to those days—something she didn't often do in her working life. "That's what I wanted to see, her really think," Streisand remembered. "And she said, 'It was wonderful . . .' And that's what's in the film."

In many of the scenes, Lauren was required to balance comedy with tender authenticity—the relationship between Rose and Hannah is in many ways the emotional heart of the movie. For both women, there were old demons to reckon with—for Streisand, the film was an opportunity to have a conversation with her own mother, with whom she had always had a troubled relationship. Lauren, in turn, was able to examine her own regrets in relation to her children. Stephen's book, *Bogart: In Search of My Father*, had just been published, shedding light on his loving but not always easy relationship with his famous mother. Some of the lines she speaks in the movie must have hit close to home: "You know parents, they don't have a plan to hurt their children. I never wanted to hurt you."

Barbra Streisand later recalled the shooting of the kitchen scene, in which the two characters are having their heartfelt talk one early morning. It is this scene that is often thought to have earned Lauren her Oscar nomination.

"After working all day, we were rehearsing a scene that we were going to shoot the next morning and I could see that she was very tired. Her hair was messy, she had a toothpick in her mouth. And I thought, this is good, this is good, keep the toothpick, this is it, let's just stay here, we'll stay a little later and get this on film right now. She said, 'But I don't know the lines yet.' And I said, 'That doesn't matter, they're on the chair over there and you can look if you need to. Meanwhile, just talk to me. Tell me what you feel. Tell me about your life now.' She started off with something like, 'I thought I was going to be young forever.' And then, by engaging her in real conversation beyond the script, the scene now had this whole other layer, about growing older. She was letting us into her life. It was a golden moment, the kind I always look for on screen. They reach out and touch everyone because they're so true."

The Mirror Has Two Faces had its glitzy premiere at the Ziegfeld Theatre in New York on November 10, 1996. Lauren arrived in the company of Stephen and looked ravishing. The star-studded audience applauded the film and the cast. It was a good night, ending with a party at Tavern on the Green. Reviews were less enthusiastic—many complained about Streisand's preoccupation with her own image, calling the film a shameless vanity project. Curiously, such complaints have rarely been expressed whenever a male actor/director undertakes a similar effort. Most critics agreed, however, that Lauren was the movie's highlight. "The film has a big asset in Ms. Bacall," stated the *New York Times*. "Though she plays a mother so targeted for disapproval that she might as well be wearing a bull's-eye on her back. Ignoring all that, and delivering her lines with trademark tart panache, Ms. Bacall cuts an elegant and sardonic figure."

From the moment the first reviews were in, Lauren became a hot favorite for award-season glory, with the press predicting she'd finally get her long overdue Academy Award nomination. During her fifty-plus-year career in movies, she had never been recognized with so much as a nomination for any of Hollywood's major awards. The oversight was seen as shocking—which, indeed, it was. In January of 1997, she picked up the Golden Globe for best supporting actress—four years after receiving the Cecil B DeMille Lifetime Achievement Award from the same organization. "It's taken me a long time to get here, but here I am, and I'm not giving it back," she joked. Unsurprisingly, when the Oscar nominations were announced later that month, she was among the five actresses nominated for a best supporting role. She was careful not to build up her expectations too high, though the truth was she wanted to win with all her heart. The media hype did little to prepare her for the possibility of failure; almost all outlets predicted her victory. Along the way, she also picked up the Screen Actors Guild Award, making the Oscar appear ever more inevitable. What Lauren and many others failed to recognize was the sheer power of Harvey Weinstein and his campaigning tactics. *The English Patient* and the 1997 awards season would be the first of Weinstein's truly "aggressive campaigns." On the evening of March 24, Lauren arrived at the ceremony, accompanied by her three children. She was nervous but looked beautiful and playful—everyone seemed certain she was the winner, not least her family. Her award was up first. Kevin Spacey, himself convinced he'd be calling Bacall's name, seemed momentarily taken aback, before announcing Juliette Binoche as the winner. Lauren quickly composed herself and smiled as she applauded, although Stephen was visibly upset.

"We got through the rest of the program and headed for the great dinner," she wrote in her memoir. "I felt very alone. No matter how you slice it, this was a ball for winners."

The Oscar loss was a great disappointment, one more proof that even after all these years, she was still not one of "them." Hollywood had been tough on her from the start. Some have suggested that Bacall's loss was due to the fact she was unpopular among the film's elite. If that's true, the same could be said for Streisand. The combination of these two independent women certainly rubbed Oscar voters the wrong way—in the end, *The Mirror Has Two Faces* garnered just two nominations (the other one being for best original song).

One of Lauren's agents, Scott Henderson, told William J. Mann: "She was devastated. I think she knew a lot of people didn't like her and didn't vote for her because of that. And that was really, really painful for her."

The blow was significantly softened later the same year when Lauren received the Kennedy Center Honors, in recognition of her "distinguished achievement in the performing arts" and her "extraordinary contributions to the life of our country." She was naturally thrilled—the timing couldn't be more perfect. She had previously participated in honoring her friends—Katharine Hepburn in 1990 and Kirk Douglas in 1994—and never expected that she'd one day be at the receiving end. The ceremony, which took place on December 7, 1997, was a happy one, with tributes from friends and colleagues and a montage of her roller-coaster life and career. The press noted that "there was an almost tangible wave of affection for Bacall" in the room—something she desperately needed after the Academy snub.

Family was now becoming increasingly important to Lauren. She had always had a tremendous amount of love for her children, but she was the first to admit that she hadn't been present enough in the past. In her role as a grandmother, she was very much the same way—loving, wise, generous, but not one to babysit or bake cookies for the little ones. Her work had always been her first love, and it continued to take the central place in her life, even in her seventies and beyond. As long as her health allowed it, she would keep herself open to offers, always ready to challenge herself, to try something new.

Opportunities for projects, some more interesting than others, kept coming her way. Before the end of the millennium, she had appeared in five more motion pictures. Her roles were small and none of the films, including *My Fellow Americans*, where she costarred with Jack Lemmon and James Garner, proved very successful, but what mattered was that she continued to keep herself busy. In 1999, she was back on Broadway one last time, starring opposite Rosemary Harris in Noel Coward's *Waiting in the Wings*. The comedy, set in a retirement home for actresses, was a moderate success. Many flocked to see the legendary Lauren Bacall live onstage, although the play, being an ensemble piece, was a far cry from the star vehicles she had headlined in the past.

There were still a handful of notable movies to come. In 2003, Lauren surprised many by accepting a role in *Dogville*, a highly experimental film by the controversial Danish director Lars von Trier. She was once again part of a large ensemble, led by Nicole Kidman, who was riding the wave of her post-divorce renaissance. Working with von Trier was a challenge for Lauren. She was asked to improvise more than she had ever done before, often instructed to just busy herself in the background, not knowing if she was being shot or not. This was the furthest she could have possibly ventured from her classic Hollywood training. Arguably no other star from the old studio system managed to make such a transition. "Lars's method involves an actor more or less forgetting what movies have taught him throughout his career," she later wrote about the experience.

When the film was released in Europe in 2003, it was praised by critics as innovative and groundbreaking. The minimalist staging, the complete lack of the usual narrative tricks used in cinema, and the subtle philosophical messages encoded into the movie all made it a favorite among highbrow critics, many of whom later included it on their lists of the year's (and subsequently the decade's) best films. US critics were considerably more divided, with many remaining skeptical about the film being anything more than a gimmick. Lauren's appearance in the film was also seen as a curiosity.

"Many of the actors seem cast for marquee value," noted one publication. "Is Lauren Bacall really the best actress to disappear into the thankless role of the town's store owner? Anyone expecting a glamorous Bacall from Hollywood's yesteryear will be clearly disappointed."

But being the "glamorous Bacall from Hollywood's yesteryear" was exactly the thing she wanted to get away from. How ridiculous it was for people to expect her to appear the same as she had sixty years prior? Bacall's aged face carried a different kind of beauty now—proudly untouched by plastic surgery, with her hair dyed a natural shade of blond-grey. "I think your whole life shows in your face and you should be proud of it," she said when asked about her lack of interest in cosmetic enhancements.

The experience of working with Lars von Trier on *Dogville* was positive enough for Lauren to return for the movie's unofficial sequel, *Manderlay*, in 2005. "As an actor, if you accept a part in a Lars von Trier movie, you don't expect to get rich," she joked. "But you do expect an interesting experience. You expect it to be original, and totally unlike anything you would find in America."

Through *Dogville*, she got to know and form a friendship with Nicole Kidman, whom she thought "not only beautiful, but very smart, very professional, and a first-class actress of broad scope." For her part, Kidman was just as impressed. "I was honored to work with her—intimidated and thrilled," she confessed. "She's incredibly strong, a great mother and a wonderful actress." There were those in the press who tried to instigate a feud between the two stars, especially after Lauren's public comments that Kidman was "not a legend." For anyone who had known Bacall and her relationship with her own "legend" status, the statement was far from derogatory. In her mind, legends were dead—Kidman was an actress at the peak of her abilities, with decades of good work ahead of her. The media's efforts to create controversy were apparently unsuccessful, as Lauren and Kidman would once again work together in Jonathan Glazer's *Birth*, released in 2004. The atmospheric, contemplative movie tells the story of a fragile young widow (Kidman) who is approached by a ten-year-old boy claiming to be her dead husband reincarnated. Bacall plays Kidman's mother, and while once again her role isn't a large one, Glazer does use her expressive face to the full effect in some of the movie's most striking close-ups. The film was yet another polarizing entry in her filmography—while some saw it as a quiet masterpiece of mood and emotion, others dismissed it. Critics were especially disturbed by the scene in which Kidman takes a naked bath with the ten-year-old Cameron Bright.

For Lauren, *Birth* was to be the last high-profile movie appearance of her career. There were still more roles to come: in 2007, she had a showy supporting role in the little-seen film, *The Walker*, in which she played a rich Washington socialite. Her few scenes with Woody Harrelson are among the film's strongest, and they demonstrate that even at eighty-two, Bacall still had the goods to steal any scene she was in. The camera still loved her, and she was able to convey more with a single glance than many younger actors could with lines and lines of dialogue.

As her health became more fragile, she was able to use her iconic voice to continue acting. She voiced the Witch of the Waste in Hayao Miyazaki's animated fantasy *Howl's Moving Castle*, which was the artist's subtly veiled critique of the US invasion of Iraq. The film was nominated for the Academy Award and has since become one of

Miyazaki's most beloved features, linking Lauren to yet another strand of film history.

She also starred in Natalie Portman's short film *Eve*, in which she played a lead role, opposite Ben Gazzara. Portman, who was trying to find her feet as a first-time director, was in awe of the legendary star, but her admiration was not fully reciprocated. "I was not decisive, and she called me out on it and was totally right. But she was a total pro, despite the fact that she was so unimpressed by me. She was amazing in every take," Portman later reflected on the experience. "She did not like me, but I loved her and admired her so much." In 2006, Bacall made a splashy cameo in *The Sopranos*, playing herself and lending her presence to the iconic series.

In 2009, she was told that the Academy was finally ready to make amends and present her with an honorary Oscar during their annual Governors Awards ceremony. It was certainly a bittersweet moment. God knows she had earned it, and yet, it also felt like an afterthought. She nonetheless looked glowing as she sat in her honorary spot, surrounded by her children. The award was presented to her by Anjelica Huston, a dear friend, of whose birth Lauren had learned all those years earlier in the middle of the jungle from her proud father, director John Huston. Anjelica's presence gave the occasion a sense of connection with the past—memories of Bogie and the old days came flooding in, so much so that when delivering her speech, Lauren forgot to mention Sam or Jason. The omission would haunt her for the rest of her life, casting a dark shadow on the entire Oscar experience. She had always felt so very close to Sam—how could she leave him out of her speech? Nerves, emotion, the heat of the moment, no doubt—and yet she found it impossible to forgive herself.

Bacall's last two movies, *Wide Blue Yonder* (also known as *All at Sea*) and *The Forger*, were both independent, low-budget productions, seen by a handful of audiences. In both, she is a delight to watch, although she is given little to do. The circle of her cinematic life was completed. *Wide Blue Yonder* would receive its delayed, limited release in the United States in June of 2014—almost exactly seventy years after *To Have and*

Have Not opened. In the wistful final scene of the movie, Lauren says her farewell to her costar, Brian Cox, before getting in a boat and slowly drifting off, smiling softly. It was a fitting, if understated way for one of cinema's grandest dames to leave the screen—her hypnotizing allure undimmed by time.

Her last professional engagement was a voice role in the "Mom's the Word" episode of Seth MacFarlane's hit animated sitcom, *Family Guy*, which aired in March 2014. Her character, an elderly friend of Peter Griffin's mother, deals with loneliness and the idea of mortality. Although framed within MacFarlane's signature satire, there is poignancy and more than a note of sadness to Lauren's performance. Her role in the show served as final proof that as an actress, she was forever willing to adapt and try new things, never allowing herself to get stuck in the hazy mist of her past glories.

After suffering a fall at her Dakota apartment in late 2010, she had difficulties walking. She managed at first by using a walker, but eventually, she became dependent on a wheelchair. Witnessing the weakening of her own body was difficult—it meant she could no longer do what she loved: work and be fully independent. She was spending most of her time at home now, surrounded by memories, by the mementos of her rich life. In 2011, she was photographed in her apartment by Annie Lebovitz. The photos were featured in a *Vanity Fair* piece about her. In the striking images, Lauren appears her usual proud self—just as alert and sharp as she had always been. Her beloved Papillon dog, Sophie, who was now her closest companion, was pictured at her side.

It was difficult not to feel alone. Leonard Bernstein had been gone since 1990. Katharine Hepburn and Gregory Peck both passed away in 2003. After Katie's death, Lauren was the last of the original celluloid goddesses still living in Manhattan.

"My son tells me, 'Do you realize you are the last one? The last person who was an eyewitness to the golden age?'" she told *Vanity Fair* in one of her last interviews. "Young people, even in Hollywood, ask me, 'Were you *really* married to Humphrey Bogart?' 'Well, yes, I think I was.'"

Yet she was far from the tragic figure some liked to paint her as. She had lived a fantastic life, filled with tremendous highs and triumphs, with joy and heartbreak, with work and friends. She had her children and grandchildren. She achieved what she had set out to, all those decades before, as she paced the pavements outside Sardis. As for happiness, "I don't think anybody that has a brain can really be happy," she reflected. "What is there really to be happy *about*? You tell me. If you're a thinking human being, there's no way to divorce yourself from the world."

The end came suddenly. She was in her apartment when a massive stroke hit. It was August 12, 2014. She was taken to New York-Presbyterian Hospital, where the following day, she died peacefully, surrounded by her three children.

"To me, a star is someone who lasts," she once said. Lauren Bacall certainly lasted. Her career spanned seventy years. She was a star with her very first movie, and upon her death, just a month before her ninetieth birthday, she was still every inch a star. Her passing was front-page news around the world: one of the last of the Golden Age greats was gone. "My obit is going to be full of Bogart, I'm sure," she said not long before her death. "I'll never know if that's true. If that's the way it is, that's the way it is." In truth, even if Bogie did feature heavily in most of the pieces published, most remembered her chiefly as a force, a strong and independent woman, an enduring star, and a gifted actress—the last certainly would have pleased her. The *Hollywood Reporter* called her "Hollywood's Icon of Cool," while the *New York Times* wrote about her "lasting mystique" which had "put her on the plateau of American culture few stars reach."

Lauren Bacall was laid to rest beside Bogie, in Forest Lawn's Garden of Memory. After more than half a century, they were reunited. The memorial service was private, with only close members of her family present. She was back in the land where she had been discovered, the place she had always been at odds with—now, forever part of its legend.

SOURCE NOTES

CHAPTER 1: BETTY

5 **"In all fairness":** Bacall, Lauren, *By Myself… And Then Some*, 7.

6 **"Your wife told me":** "Another Side of the Bacall Story," *Los Angeles Times*, February 19, 1979, 55.

6 **"From the day…":** "Another Side of the Bacall Story," 55.

6 **"She never tried":** *By Myself*, 5.

6 **"When her play":** *Los Angeles Times*.

7 **"I asked how":** "Bewitched by Lauren Bacall," *Washington Post*, August 13, 2014.

9 **"I had my first":** *By Myself*, 13.

10 **"No crown of diamonds":** *By Myself*, 20.

10 **"My days":** *By Myself*, 23.

10 **"marvellous":** *By Myself*, 26.

12 **"But it was":** *By Myself*, 34.

13 **"She came into my office":** *Diana Vreeland: The Eye Has to Travel* documentary, 2011.

13 **"definitely an original":** *By Myself*, 72.

14 **"very charming":** *By Myself*, 71.

14 **"basket case":** *By Myself*, 74.

14 **"You can't get":** Multiple sources, including "Behind the Scenes with Louise Dahl-Wolfe," Fashion Studies, December 2018. https://www.fashionstudies.ca/behind-the-scenes.

14 **"Betty was great":** *Diana Vreeland: The Eye Has to Travel.*

14 **"None of it":** Michael Parkinson, "Lauren Bacall on Parkinson," 1979. BBC/YouTube. https://www.youtube.com/watch?v=iW3WLUzUyk8.

CHAPTER 2: THE WHISTLE HEARD AROUND THE WORLD

18 **"Ernest, you're a damn fool":** "There's Something about Harry: To Have and Have Not as Novel and Film," *Bright Lights Film Journal*, August 1, 1999.

22 **“I liked him immediately”:** *By Myself*, 98.

22 **“And don’t tell”:** *By Myself*, 101.

22 **“She just sounds”:** A. M. Sperber and Eric Lax, *Bogart* (1997), 328.

24 **“she talked way down”:** *Bogart*, 329.

25 **“I want to put you”:** Multiple sources, including Lauren Bacall interview on Michael Parkinson, 1979.

25 **“Come with me”:** Todd McCarthy, *Howard Hawks: The Grey Fox of Hollywood*, (2000), 224.

26 **“There was no clap of thunder”:** *By Myself*, 112.

27 **“She’s a secret”:** “And Betty Bacall Also Has a New First Name,” *The Record*, April 22, 1944, 13.

29 **“I found out very quickly”:** *By Myself*, 118.

30 **“When the picture is over”:** *Bogart*, 120.

31 **“What kind of”:** *Bogart*, 120.

CHAPTER 3: BOGIE AND BACALL

32 **“Volumes have been”:** “Lauren Bacall, Newest Screen Siren, Different, *Evening Star*, November 5, 1944, 45.

32 **“Lauren Bacall has cinema personality”:** “Cinema: The New Pictures,” *Time*, October 23, 1944.

32 **“one of the great”:** *Life*, June 12, 1945.

32 **“Bacall Cult”:** “New Star May Become Hub of Cult,” *Fort Worth Star Telegram*, November 7, 1944, 14.

35 **“Beware of Mayo”:** Jonathan Ross, “Lauren Bacall: *Hollywood Greats*,” 2005. BBC/YouTube. https://www.youtube.com/watch?v=1MALKWGpkto.

35 **“We had some bumpy”:** Lauren Bacall interview for *Hollywood Greats*.

35 **“I have told Mayo”:** Joe Hyams, *Bogie: The Humphery Bogart Story*, 86.

37 **“Where are you coming from?”:** *Lauren Bacall: Face to Face*, 1995. BBC/YouTube. https://www.youtube.com/watch?v=uR_lpSY5qUc&t=1924s.

37 **“I learned to . . .”:** *Lauren Bacall: Face to Face*.

38 **“He’s very cute about it”:** *By Myself*, 178.

40 **“From the moment”:** “Boyer Steals Lauren’s Show,” *Des Moines Register*, December 14, 1945, 12.

40 **“If I had the care”:** Mark Cousins, “Lauren Bacall: Scene by Scene,” YouTube. https://www.youtube.com/watch?v=gtoHk6qDncE&t=20s.

41 **“We had made a pact”:** Lauren Bacall, *Face to Face*, BBC.

42 **“the mood of”:** “Dark Passage Opens at Strand,” *New York Times*, September 6, 1947.

43 **“John was wonderful”:** Cousins, “Lauren Bacall.”

45 **“This has nothing to do”:** Sourced from “Blacklist: The Hollywood Red Scare,” exhibition at the Jewish Museum, Los Angeles, July 2023.

45 **“Why I Came to Washington”:** published in *Washington Daily News*, October 29, 1947.

45 **"we certainly were naïve":** *By Myself*, 201.
45 **"I was so in awe of him":** Charlie Rose, "Lauren Bacall Interviewed on Charlie Rose," 1994, YouTube. https://www.youtube.com/watch?v=GaqwNIak470.
46 **"I'm a liberal":** Rose, "Lauren Bacall Interviewed."
47 **"The really ungrateful role":** "It's a Long, Wistful Road Trumpet Geniuses Travel," *Evening Star*, March 10, 1950, 63.
47 **"Everyone thought":** *By Myself*, 223.

CHAPTER 4: UNCONVENTIONAL MOVIE STAR

52 **"just how desperately":** *Now*, 123.
52 **"I was selfish":** *By Myself*, 233.
53 **"Times have changed":** "Many Chances for Cutie to Make a Fortune," *Ottawa Citizen*, March 28, 1953, 39.
54 **"Grable and I":** *By Myself*, 233.
54 **"not easy":** *By Myself*, 233.
54 **"She was sweet":** Lauren Bacall interview with Robert Osborne, 2005. YouTube.
54 **"impressive artistic":** "Story of Three Beauties is Artistic Achievement," *Buffalo Express*, November 11, 1953.
54 **"an average":** "Trio of stars in Cinemascope," *New York Times*, November 11, 1953.
55 **"Miss Bacall":** "Little Story in Millionaire (But the Gals!)," *Des Maines Tribune*, November 23, 1953.
55 **"I don't like the moments":** Parkinson, "Lauren Bacall on Parkinson."
56 **"after eight years":** *By Myself*, 236.
56 **"After we were":** Mavis Nicholson, "Lauren Bacall: Interview on Afternoon Plus," Channel 4, 1985. YouTube. https://www.youtube.com/watch?v=zmncBWospE0.
57 **"unforgettables":** *By Myself*, 240.
57 **"loving the chance":** *By Myself*, 240.
57 **"I have admiration":** "Sidney Skolsky: Hollywood is My Beast," *LA Evening Citizen News*, December 2, 1953, 10.
58 **"the first and only":** *By Myself*, 245.
61 **"Of course, it's about":** Lauren Bacall letter, August 20, 1954. Mankiewicz Papers.
61 **"It was a part":** *Now*, 116.
62 **"I was a romantic":** *Now*, 116.
63 **"Bacall is charming":** *The Noel Coward Diaries* (1992), 224.

CHAPTER 5: THE MOST FAMOUS WIDOW IN THE WORLD

65 **"Bacall's worst nightmare":** "Bogie & Me," *The Guardian*. https://www.theguardian.com/film/2008/feb/10/news.usa.
66 **"drove Mitchum to quit":** Aissa Wayne, *John Wayne: My Father*, 173.

68 **"sleepwalked through":** "Sexual frustration and visual excess: Laura Mulvey on Douglas Sirk's *Written on the Wind*." Sourced from bfi.org. https://www.bfi.org.uk/sight-and-sound/features/sexual-frustration-visual-excess-laura-mulvey-douglas-sirks-written-wind.

68 **"You better see":** *By Myself*, 255.

69 **"I should have":** *By Myself*, 255.

70 **"escaping from":** *By Myself*, 255.

70 **"probably the world's":** "Hollywood's Rat Pack Is Exclusive Too," *Salina Journal*, November 12, 1956, 8.

70 **"I think we should":** Hollywood's Rat Pack Is Exclusive Too," 8.

72 **"the screen's first":** "This and That in Movieland," *Wichita Eagle*, September 9, 1956, 100.

72 **"Aside from her professionalism":** TCM, "Gregory Peck Tribute to Lauren Bacall." TCM archives.

73 **"Goodbye, Spence":** Joe Hyams, *Bogie: The Humphery Bogart Story*, 168.

74 **"Mrs. Bogart, it's all over":** *By Myself*, 290.

74 **"one of the largest":** "Final Tribute Paid Bogart in Filmland," *Columbus Enquirer*, January 18, 1957, 22.

75 **"In spite of the":** Letter quoted in *By Myself*, 305.

76 **"There's real chemistry'":** *Going Ons About Town*. https://www.newyorker.com/goings-on-about-town/movies/designing-woman.

76 **"Excellent":** "Designing Woman," *Variety*, December 31, 1956.

76 **"This time Lauren Bacall":** "Lauren Bacall Scores in Designing Woman," *Valley Times*, April 11, 1957, 27.

77 **"I wanted it all":** *By Myself*, 313.

77 **"She is witty, gay":** "Lauren Bacall and Frank Sinatra Are a Tear-Dimmed Couple," *Tampa Tribune*, November 24, 1957.

77 **"I didn't really know":** *By Myself*, 315.

78 **"Every so often":** "Miss Bacall Impressive in Gift of Love Film," *Richmond News Reader*, April 20, 1958, 46.

CHAPTER 6: WELCOME TO THE THEATER

79 **"That trip":** *By Myself*, 326.

80 **"There comes a time":** "Lauren Cuts Last Tie with the Past," *Daily Mirror*, September 30, 1958, 19.

81 **"one of the most desirable":** More Kenneth, *More or Less*, 178.

81 **"needs constant":** "Jumpin" Juipur!," April 19, 1959, 21.

81 **"She just went down":** "Lauren Fainted from REAL Terror," *Sunday People*, October 11, 1959, 18.

83 **"far-out":** *Now*, 113.

84 **"For the first time":** *By Myself*, 336.

84 **"For a woman":** *By Myself*, 335.
84 **"from that night":** *By Myself*, 336.
84 **"Ms. Bacall is":** "Lauren Bacall at Nixon in a Brand New Play," *Pittsburgh Post-Gazette*, October 20, 1959, 27.
85 **"Mr. Hayword":** "Lauren Bacall at Nixon in a Brand New Play," 27.
85 **"Ms. Bacall plays":** "Bacall and Chaplin Delightful But "Charlie" Dwindles Away," *Daily News*, December 17, 1959, 74.
86 **"I wasn't truly":** *By Myself*, 345.
86 **"The Lauren Bacall-Jason Robards palship":** "Earl Wilson Says," *News and Observer*, September 15, 1960, 6.
89 **"In all this confusion":** "'Shock' Film Melodramatic," *News Journal*, May 1, 1964, 32.
92 **"Just when I thought":** "Her Famous Line Isn't Forgotten Yet," *Quad City Times*, April 8, 1966, 25.
92 **"It's the calm":** "'Harper" Rugged Adventure with Bacall, Newman," *Miami News*, April 7, 1966, 13.
92 **"Miss Bacall is her usual":** "He Tried for Bogart but Looks Like 007," *New York Times News Service*, April 1, 1966, 13.
92 **"When you look":** *Miami News*.
92 **"After all":** "Bogeyland's Back Death to Spies!," *Reading Evening Post*, January 18, 1966, 2.

CHAPTER 7: A STAR IS REBORN

93 **"I've lived with one":** *Now*, 124.
94 **"I felt I had value":** *By Myself*, 363.
94 **"I don't know":** Mann, *Bogie and Bacall*, 499.
94 **"Thanks to the rare":** "Cactus Flower Beats Doldrums," *Pittsburgh Press*, May 29, 1966, 69.
95 **"You can't do much better":** "Cactus Flower Beats Doldrums," 69.
96 **"That's the way":** *Now*, 133.
97 **"I had never worked":** *By Myself*, 404.
97 **"Miss Bacall is a sensation":** "Lauren Bacall in Applause," *New York Times*, March 31, 1970, 35.
98 **"Miss Bacall is the most stylish":** "Miss Bacall in Applause Helps to Nourish Season," *Standard Star*, March 31, 1970, 27.
99 **"Miss Bacall sidesteps":** "Bacall Takes Your Breath Away," *New York Times*, April 5, 1970, 93.
99 **"remarkable" and "splendid":** "Applause Review," *New York Post*, March 31, 1970.
99 **"We can't understand":** "Lauren Bacall Sparks Applause," *Windsor Star*, February 21, 1970, 39.
100 **"I feel, for the first time":** "Bravo Applause of Lauren Bacall," *Denville Register and Bee*, May 10, 1970, 37.

101 **"She had never":** "Len Cariou Interview at BroadwayCon 2020." YouTube. https://www.youtube.com/watch?v=vwE-SWWem44.

101 **"No one but you":** *By Myself*, 417.

102 **"If any musical":** "One Hand Clapping," *The Observer*, November 19, 1972, 37.

104 **"In updating":** "Lauren Bacall in a Not So Wonderful Show," *The Dispatch*, February 11, 1981, 91.

104 **"The only reason":** "Lauren Bacall in a Not So Wonderful Show," 91.

104 **"I wrote the book":** "Stage: Lauren Bacall in Woman of the Year," *New York Times*, March 30, 1981, 15.

105 **"Listen, I'm":** "Lauren Bacall's Glamour, Grit and Gutsy Candour," *Boston Globe*, February 1, 1981, 91.

CHAPTER 8: LADY IN DISTRESS

106 **"When you're in":** *Now*, 142.

106 **"I have not been":** Dick Cavett, "Lauren Bacall 'I'm on the Wrong Show," *The Dick Cavett Show*, April 28, 1971. YouTube. https://www.youtube.com/watch?v=miorylnw6Ag.

107 **"When you're in":** *Now*, 142.

107 **"Bacall was bigger":** "The Shadows of Lauren Bacall," *New Yorker*, August 13, 2014.

108 **"The cast were all":** "How We Made the Original *Murder on the Orient Express*," *The Guardian*, November 13, 2017.

108 **"the happiest movie experience":** *By Myself*, 375.

108 **"They all did it for Sidney":** "How We Made the Original *Murder on the Orient Express*," *The Guardian*, November 13, 2017.

109 **"I thought it would be . . .":** Sidney Lumet Interview for the Feature *Making Murder on the Orient Express: The Players*. YouTube. https://www.youtube.com/watch?v=RhSPBsp3pFE&t=14s.

110 **"basically alone":** "Having Survived the Tempest of Life with a Famous Mom and Dad, Actor Sam Sets Sail on His Own," *People*, October 18, 1982.

111 **"I could totally disagree":** *Now*, 112.

112 **"John Wayne was no longer":** "Hec Ramsey & The Shootist with co-star Rick Lenz," *A Word on Westerns*. May 15, 2018. YouTube. https://www.youtube.com/watch?v=vBevLvPoC9Q.

112 **"If *The Shootist* . . .":** "Shootist Somehow Misses the Mark," *Chicago Tribune*, September 20, 1976.

112 **"I'm so fed up . . .":** Nicholson, "Lauren Bacall: Interview on Afternoon Plus."

113 **"The chronology is there":** "Here's Another One You Read Earlier," *The Guardian*, March 20, 2005.

114 **"I was very excited":** "The Ultimate Michael Biehn Interview," *Den of Geek*, August 30, 2011.

115 **"I thought that she was":** "The Ultimate Michael Biehn Interview."

116 **"The movie I wanted":** *People*, June 1981.

117 **"The ghouls are outside":** *People*.

117 **"I think it's disgusting":** *People*.

117 **"*The Fan* has several terrific things":** "Film: 'Fan,' A Lauren Bacall Thriller," *New York Times*, May 22, 1981.

117 **"I think I'll run away":** *People*, June 1981.

CHAPTER 9: AT HOME

119 **"There is no way":** "Lauren Bacall's Idol," *Los Angeles Times*, November 3, 2014.

120 **"As anyone can see":** From the French *Vogue* interview, quoted in the Lauren Bacall Collection Catalogue, Bonhams.

121 **"What bugs me":** "Lauren Bacall's Glamour, Grit and Gutsy Candour," *Boston Globe*, February 1, 1981, 91.

122 **"The question remains":** "How Long Can Lauren Bacall Hold Up a Disaster," *San Francisco Examiner*, April 19, 1981, 266.

122 **"It is my feeling":** Johnny Carson, "Lauren Bacall interview on the *Johnny Carson Show*," June 23, 1983. YouTube. https://www.youtube.com/watch?v=5BTJ314dspo.

122 **"To Bogie she was":** "The Long Goodbye by Rex Reed," *The Observer*, July 1, 2015.

123 **"not overtly friendly":** Michael Michaud interview with author, September 20, 2023.

124 **"A handful":** Nat Segaloff interview with author, December 2023.

124 **"She could certainly be":** Fred Goldrich interview with author, January 2019.

125 **"I don't pay attention":** Lauren Bacall, Merv Griffin interview, 1987. YouTube.

126 **"When I started to play":** *Now*, 145–46.

126 **"It was Lauren Bacall":** "The Lauren Bacall I Knew," *The Times*, August 14, 2014.

127 **"Oh, Harold is":** "Lauren Bacall Walks the Walk," *Live Journal*, December 22, 2007.

127 **"To watch this lady":** Mike Allen, *Plymouth Sound Radio*. haroldpinter.org.

127 **"Slinky as a lynx":** "Essence of Williams," *The Observer*, July 14, 1985, 70.

127 **"I've never seen":** "From the archive: When Melvyn Brugg Met Lauren Bacall," *The Guardian*, July 20, 2019.

128 **"Well, how are you":** "Bacall Better than Bogie," *Sydney Morning Herald*, January 11, 1986, 1.

128 **"I just disembarked":** "News: Lauren Bacall," 1986, ABC Library. YouTube. https://www.youtube.com/watch?v=bwBeN8zoPk4.

128 **"I think I was":** *Now*, 148.

129 **"I don't understand":** "Face to Face," 1995, BBC.

129 **"Playing it broadly":** "An Invitation to Dinner," *Daily News*, December 11, 1989, 76.

130 **"I don't get many":** "The Allure of Lauren Bacall," *The Tennessean*, March 9, 1991, 27.

131 **"I've known Betty":** "Peck, Bacall Reunite for The Portrait," *New Journal*, February 13, 1993, 46.

CHAPTER 10: CURTAIN CALL

132 **"She never got":** "Lauren Bacall, Hollywood's Icon of Cool Dies at 89," *Hollywood Reporter*, August 12, 2014.

133 **"As I headed for":** *By Myself*, 438.

134 **"Lauren had":** Barbra-archives.info. https://www.barbra-archives.info/the-mirror-has-two-faces-1996-movie.

134 **"They ought to":** "Liz Smith: The Punch Hunt is On," *Newsday*, September 5, 1995, 13.

134 **"I always saw":** Nicholson, "Lauren Bacall: Interview on Afternoon Plus."

135 **"Wonderful, wonderful":** Barbra-archives.info.

135 **"After working":** Barbra-archives.info.

136 **"The film has":** "Streisand on Topic A," *New York Times*, November 15, 1996.

137 **"We got through":** *By Myself*, 443.

137 **"She was devastated":** quoted in Mann, *Bogie and Bacall*, 541.

137 **"distinguished":** *By Myself*, 444.

138 **"there was almost":** "Dylan to Heston," *Richmond Times*, December 9, 1997, 35.

139 **"Lars's method":** *By Myself*, 477.

139 **"Many of the actors":** "Controversial 'Dogville' Opens at Harvard Exit," *Seattle Gay News*, April 16, 2004, 34.

139 **"I think your whole life":** "Lauren Bacall: Hollywood's Most Beautiful Face," *The Guardian*, August 30, 2014.

139 **"As an actor":** Closer Interview with Lauren Bacall. YouTube.

139 **"Not only beautiful":** *By Myself*, 474.

140 **"I was honored":** "To Have and Have Not," *Vanity Fair*, March 2011.

141 **"I was not decisive":** "She was unimpressed by me," *Daily Mail*, August 20, 2016.

142 **"My son tells me":** "To Have and Have Not," *Vanity Fair*, March 2011.

143 **"I don't think":** "To Have and Have Not."

143 **"To me, a star":** Parkinson, "Lauren Bacall on Parkinson."

143 **"My obit":** "To Have and Have Not," *Vanity Fair*, March 2011.

143 **"Hollywood's Icon of Cool":** "Lauren Bacall, Hollywood's Icon of Cool Dies at 89," *Hollywood Reporter*, August 12, 2014.

143 **"lasting mystique":** "Lauren Bacall Dies at 89; in a Bygone Hollywood, She Purred Every Word," *New York Times*, August 12, 2014.

INDEX

ABOUT THE AUTHOR

Photo courtesy of the author

Anthony Uzarowski is a writer and film historian with a keen interest in classical Hollywood. His previous books include the acclaimed biographies of Ava Gardner and Jessica Lange, and his writings on cinema, travel, and the arts has appeared in numerous publications including *The Guardian, Air Mail, Turner Classic Movies, The Gay Times*, and *Film International*. Uzarowski holds degrees in languages and film studies from University College London.